"I grew up believing and repeating the mantra that God is more interested in our holiness than our happiness. But that idea reduces both holiness and happiness. The more profound truth, which Barnabas Piper so capably puts forth in this engaging and accessible book, is that growth in genuine holiness gives us the freedom to pursue profound and eternal happiness."

Nancy Guthrie, Author,
God Does His Best Work with Empty

"It takes a bold soul to talk about happiness these days. What is it? Can we attain it? Is it ok to desire it? Will it last? Perhaps most important of all, does God want us to be happy? Barnabas Piper accepts the challenge to answer such questions and does a remarkably good job of it. There is an "earthy" realism in this book that is also profoundly spiritual and biblical. In speaking of happiness, Piper isn't naïve, nor is he oblivious to heartache, disappointment, and pain. But he is confident in the goodness of God and the trustworthy nature of his promises. Did reading this book make me happy? Well, yes, it did! Highly recommended."

Sam Storms, Author; Senior Pastor, Bridgeway Church,
Oklahoma City, OK

"Who of us doesn't want to be happy? But happiness is hard to find and hard to hold on to. Barnabas Piper's new book, *Hoping for Happiness,* guides us gently away from frowning religiosity and away from giggly frivolity. Barnabas helps us toward Jesus, who overflows with happiness on offer to disappointed people who are trying to figure life out—which is every one of us."

Ray Ortlund, Renewal Ministries, Nashville

"The pursuit of happiness, which some have called an 'inalienable' human right, can be painfully elusive. We chase happiness in all sorts of things, whether it be sex, money, power, food, fitness, career, religion, or some other good thing. But with so many good things at our disposal, why is happiness still so hard to find? In this helpful volume, Barnabas answers the question by helping us see that our enjoyment of good things is not the problem. Rather, the problem is our tendency to take good things and cling to them as ultimate things. In the tradition of St. Augustine, he reminds us of how hearts are restless until they find their rest in Christ. But in Christ, as the Scripture attests, there are pleasures forevermore."

Scott Sauls, Senior Pastor, Christ Presbyterian Church, Nashville, Tennessee; Author, *Jesus Outside the Lines* and *A Gentle Answer*

"Somehow Barnabas Piper manages to cover nearly all that matters in life within the pages of this slim volume. Filled with the kind of common sense that isn't common enough, yet at the same time turning some conventional thinking on its head, *Hoping for Happiness* manages to be philosophical, pastoral, and practical all at once."

Karen Swallow Prior, Author, *On Reading Well: Finding the Good Life Through Great Books* and *Fierce Convictions: The Extraordinary Life of Hannah More—Poet, Reformer, Abolitionist*

"I loved this book. The writing is so good, but what I find most special about *Hoping for Happiness* is the humility with which Barnabas communicates. Reading it felt like being served, and every page was a loving push toward the cross. We all want to be happy. We all want to hold on to happiness. This book is an excellent help."

Scarlet Hiltibidal, Author, *Afraid of All the Things* and *He Numbered the Pores on My Face*

"We live in a sad time, among a people who are, it seems, divided between the downcast and the outraged. How, then, can one pursue happiness? That's the question Barnabas Piper tackles in this book. With his skillful clarity and creativity (as always), Piper leads us to what it might mean to be a people surprised by joy and surprised to be happy at last. Read happily."

Russell Moore, President, The Ethics & Religious Liberty Commission of the Southern Baptist Convention

"Much of my life has been spent chasing the next... (fill in the blank). Achievement. Experience. Feeling of that fleeting euphoria associated with being 'happy.' Before I met Jesus, I satiated this ache with relative impunity, fearing only the loss of what the next moment had to offer. After meeting Jesus, and particularly because of the tribe in which I found myself, eternal joy replaced 'fleeting and fickle' pleasures, and with it came a deep sense of guilt for enjoying anything about life. It has taken several years for me to be free to live and actually enjoy the temporal pleasures of this life relieved of either hedonism or shame. For these reasons and more, this book speaks to me and moves me at a core level. I believe it will do the same for all of us, no matter where we are on the spectrum in our pursuit of happy."

Léonce B. Crump Jr., Author, *Renovate*; Founder, Renovation Church

"Have you ever wondered if God actually cares if you are happy or not? In this book, *Hoping for Happiness*, Barnabas walks us all through what happiness actually means and looks like. Don't worry; it's good news. And—spoiler alert—yes, God cares about our happiness!"

Jamie Ivey, Author; Host, "The Happy Hour with Jamie Ivey" podcast

"For as long as I've known Barnabas, he has always lived what he writes, because he writes what he lives. *Hoping for Happiness* is Barnabas at his best: authentic, biblical, candid, and practical. He invites readers into the highs and lows of life, using Scripture as our necessary framework for navigating through every season. This work will help you find more realistic expectations, all the while seeing that it is possible to find happiness."

D. A. Horton, Author, *Intensional*;
Assistant Professor of Intercultural Studies,
California Baptist University

"Barnabas Piper's book, *Hoping for Happiness,* combines biblical truth with practical wisdom to help us experience true happiness. We often try to squeeze happiness out of good things in life, like family, friends, marriage, or even church. But Barnabas shows us why this is wrongheaded and how we can find true happiness under the lordship of Christ."

Preston Sprinkle, President, The Center for Faith,
Sexuality and Gender

"In a cultural moment when many of us have realized we're drowning in unhappiness, Barnabas Piper's book is the life raft we need. With clarity and compassion, Barnabas explores what true happiness looks like in reality. This book is so packed with wisdom and insight that it has the power to get us safely back to the solid ground of Christ-centered happiness."

Sammy Rhodes, Author, *Broken and Beloved*

"Countless people are trying to quench their thirst for happiness with pursuits that over-promise and under-deliver. In this timely book, Barnabas Piper points us to a divine well of happiness that will never run dry."

Costi W. Hinn, Pastor; Author, *God, Greed, and the (Prosperity) Gospel*

BARNABAS PIPER

HOPING

FOR

HAPPINESS

thegoodbook
COMPANY

Hoping for Happiness
© Barnabas Piper, 2020.

Published by:
The Good Book Company

thegoodbook.com | www.thegoodbook.co.uk
thegoodbook.com.au | thegoodbook.co.nz | thegoodbook.co.in

Published in association with the literary agency of Wolgemuth & Associates, Inc.

ISBN: 9781784984755 | Printed in Turkey

Design by André Parker

This book is dedicated to Immanuel Church of Nashville.

If I tried to name the individual people who have poured the hope and life of Jesus into me and into these pages, I would have to add whole chapters. Instead I will simply say thank you for your consistent, persistent dedication to walking in the light, outdoing one another in showing honor, welcoming one another as Christ has welcomed us, and showing me that there was hope and happiness to be had when I was at my most weary.

May the words of this book give to you some of the blessings you have shared with me.

CONTENTS

FOREWORD

BY RANDY ALCORN

Spoiler alert: I loved *Hoping for Happiness*.

Barnabas Piper hooked me when he said, "One of the main reasons I wrote this book is because I was tired of wrestling with guilt over having fun and enjoying myself. It seemed strange that God would give so many wonderful gifts only for me to feel guilty for enjoying them."

I grew up in a home with no knowledge of Jesus or the good news. I was often unhappy, spending night after night listening to music that promised happiness but failed to deliver it. Gazing at the night sky through my telescope, I longed for a connection to the wonders of the universe but couldn't find one. When I was in high school, Jesus drew me to himself. Everyone—and first of all my mom—noticed the change. The most obvious difference? I became much happier.

I loved my first-ever church, but it struck me as strange when the pastor said, "God doesn't want you happy; he wants you holy." Well, I was holier than I'd ever been, but I was much happier too. Was something wrong with me?

That wonderful pastor often cited Oswald Chambers' great book *My Utmost for His Highest*, which I eagerly read. But at the time I didn't know enough to disagree when Chambers said, "Joy should not be confused with happiness. In fact, it is an insult to Jesus Christ to use the word happiness in connection with Him."

I certainly didn't want to insult Jesus by saying he was happy or he made me happy! And I couldn't for the life of me figure out the difference between joy and happiness. (In fact, they are synonyms for everyone except Christians who've been taught otherwise.)

After a steady diet of such teaching, I became wary of happiness. Had I seen this book, *Hoping for Happiness*, back then, I'd have thought, "We shouldn't hope for what God doesn't want us to have." I'd never have believed that I'd one day write a book titled *Does God Want Us to Be Happy?* And I would have assumed the answer must be a resounding no!

Like Barnabas, I felt guilty for being happy. The message seemed to be "You could impress God if you chose a life of miserable holiness." It took me decades to realize that this wasn't merely a misguided and thoroughly unbiblical idea; it was a lie from the pit of hell. It undermined the "good news of happiness" (Isaiah 52:7, ESV, NASB).

Barnabas writes, "Everyone, whether they believe in God or not, has a deep internal yearning for eternal significance and happiness." That's why it's counterintuitive and counterproductive to pit happiness and holiness against each other. Jesus himself, the holiest human there's ever been, was the life and soul of the parties he got invited to. (His first miracle was to rescue a wedding celebration that ran out of wine.) Children loved him. Had he been stern and unhappy, they wouldn't have.

Instead of "don't seek happiness"—a command impossible to obey anyway—why not "seek your primary happiness in Jesus, and fully enjoy the derivative happiness in his countless gifts, including family, friends, food, work and play"?

We love and serve one who reveals himself as a "happy God" ("blessed," 1 Timothy 1:11; 6:15). We are to put our hope in "God, who richly provides us with everything to enjoy" (1 Timothy 6:17).

Barnabas calls on us to see God as "a generous Father, who showers you with good things day by day and invites you to enjoy them freely, daily, for your pleasure."

The years I devoted to researching and writing various books on happiness were life-changing. I discovered Scripture speaks of exactly what I'd experienced: not a flimsy superficial optimism but a happiness that's biblically grounded in the rock of Christ's blood-bought promises.

Truth is, the good news should leak into every aspect of our lives, even if we're not consciously talking about God or witnessing to someone. The "good news of happiness" should permeate our lives with, well, happiness. True holiness is happy-making, and all ultimate happiness is holy-making.

Barnabas couldn't be more right when he says, "A laughing Christian who relishes good things is a compelling, magnetic Christian—the kind who draws people to truth."

This echoes what J. C. Ryle wrote 150 years ago:

> *"It is a positive misfortune to Christianity when a Christian cannot smile. A merry heart, and a readiness to take part in all innocent mirth, are gifts of inestimable value. They go far to soften prejudices, to take stumbling blocks out of the way, and to make way for Christ and the gospel."*

There is no greater draw to the gospel than happy Christians who are full of grace and truth, quick to laugh and quick to weep for and comfort those who suffer.

My wife, Nanci, and I have been married for 43 years. In the last three, as we have faced her cancer together, we have found a deeper happiness in God and each other than ever before. We have known firsthand the "hopeful, grounded realism" that Barnabas writes of. Trusting in Jesus has brought us great happiness in him, even amid suffering and the threat of death.

In this delightful book, you'll see that Barnabas loves Jesus, family, sports, food, fun, God's creation, and life in general. So do I. We don't pass our peaks in this life. We don't even begin to reach them. A new earth awaits us. I envision Christ's laugh will be the loudest and longest at all those great feasts ahead of us. But why wait? Why not front-load our eternal happiness into our here-and-now and give ourselves and others a taste of heaven?

Hoping for Happiness says, "Hang your happiness on the right hooks, hang your hopes on God's promises, fear him, and obey his commands—and in this you'll find happiness, now and forever."

I know how good this book is. I've read it. Now it's your turn!

RANDY ALCORN
Founder and Director, Eternal Perspective Ministries;
Author, *Does God Want Us to Be Happy?*

INTRODUCTION

Is happiness possible?

When I began writing this book, the answer to that question seemed like a fairly obvious "yes." I could look up from my laptop as I wrote in coffee shops and see a world full of happy people. Across the table from me a young couple would talk softly and giggle occasionally. They seemed happy. Outside, gaggles of bachelorette partygoers moseyed along the downtown Nashville streets, combining enthusiastic off-key warbling with copious adult-beverage consumption. They seemed happy. My daughters planned sleepovers with friends, complete with movies, junk food, crafts, and very little of the aforementioned sleep. They were so happy. At the end of each week we'd head to church to worship and be refreshed and encouraged. It was a happy time.

Shortly after I turned the manuscript in, however, the COVID-19 pandemic swept the world, and all that disappeared in the space of weeks. Thousands upon thousands of people died, and the workings of entire nations ground to a halt. It was terrifying and overwhelming. Never in our collective lifetime had we faced such uncertainty. Happiness was lost for some, called into question by many, and redefined for others.

In the aftermath of a global pandemic, the answer to the question "Is happiness possible?" might sound a little different. When I set out to write this book, I thought I might have to persuade some readers to reconsider their definition of happiness—to rattle some cages and show how fleeting our sources of happiness are—before offering hope and direction. Now few of us need to be persuaded that so many of the things we look to for happiness are actually rather fragile. But more than ever, we need to know what true happiness is and how to find a version of it that cannot be shaken.

So let me begin by saying this: YES, happiness is possible. That is what this book is about—to help you find your way to a true, lasting, grounded sense of happiness. But it also seeks to answer some of those other questions that have bubbled to the surface: the ones we probably should have been asking before our worlds were rattled and that we can hardly ignore any longer.

If happiness is so attainable, why are our lives marked by such a desperate search for it? Why are we so often unsatisfied, grasping at what is next, groping for what is better, and racing after what is new and undiscovered? Why is it that even while we are in the midst of pleasure we are thinking of the *next* pleasure? It's an exhausting way to live.

But let me reassure you: this book is not going to tell you to stop pursuing happiness. That would be like saying, "Give up on life." Nor am I going to tell you to just look ahead to future joy with Christ and find all your happiness there. That would be to diminish the value of all that God has given us in the present. Instead, I'm going to show you a third option that exists in the tension between those two extremes. We must neither be so dedicated to earthly happiness as to never attain infinite joy nor so "heavenly-minded" as to be no earthly good. Both errors disconnect us from the real stuff and substance of life as God intends us to live it.

In this book, the first four chapters are, in essence, clearing the ground, helping us to see why happiness often proves elusive. Having done that, we'll be in a position to put in place the building blocks of a better, firmer, more stable kind of happiness.

I am slowly learning to take hold of this right kind of happiness. It would be gross arrogance to say I have "arrived." But I am learning, mistake by mistake—with my failures in view but my eyes fixed on Jesus—more of what it means to be truly happy. As you read this book, I hope that you too will discover a perspective that leads you to a new kind of happiness—a grounded and hopeful sort. I hope you'll escape the frenzied pursuit of the next source of happiness and relish the ones God has given you, with an eye toward what he will give you forever and ever.

Yes, you can be happy.

CHAPTER 1

LIVING THE DREAM

From the beginning of time, people have been chasing dreams.

In years gone by the dream might have been a patch of land to farm where a person could raise a family, earn a living, and die in peace. Or to "go west, young man" and stake a claim. For others it was to make it in the big city and to bask in the electric glow of industrial stability. Bohemian types dreamt of becoming artists and creators who could write and sing and give voice to truth. Still others spent their lives fighting for the dream of a free society of equals, where every person could enjoy all the rights and privileges they were due.

Over time the dream became decidedly more domesticated and suburban. Instead of a rural spread, people wanted a house, a spouse, a dog, a car, and 1.5 kids. They wanted a fair wage, weekends off, and chicken on Sundays. They wanted the home team to win, cold drinks on summer days, meat on the grill, and a yard full of friends. They wanted to send their kids to college and see them do something productive with their lives, as measured in dollars or babies.

So what about now? Maybe those nostalgic descriptions sound like the kind of life you want today. Or maybe they feel like harkening back to the myth of the "good ol' days," which never really existed except in our collective memory.

While the *shape* of our dreams may have changed since yesteryear, the *feel* of our dreams has not: we all want to be happy. It is baked into the human psyche.

Some people are thrill-seekers; others are homebodies. Some people are loners; others love big families or communities. Some people express creatively; others consume what is created. Some sing; others listen to music. Some cook; others are foodies. And some people have tried it all. No matter what, all people desire to feel happy.

So if we were trying to sketch a portrait of "the American dream" in the 21st century, what would it look like? It would be fair to say that two of the most common avenues through which people pursue happiness are work and relationships. People want work that matters and relationships that fulfill.

TODAY'S DREAMS: WORK THAT MATTERS

Several years ago I was at a friend's house one evening with a couple of other guys I didn't know. We got to talking about work, since that's the safest and most neutral conversation territory (unless you find out one of you is a pastor or in politics). They asked me what I did, and I told them that I was in marketing for a publishing company. My description must have lacked some pep though because one of the men asked me, "Do you love your job?" I answered that I was satisfied in my work and grateful for my position. His response was "Man, if you don't *love* your job, you should quit and go find something else."

On one level, it sounds like inspirational, life-changing advice. But just notice what his words reveal. He believes that the only work worth doing is work that you love. In his view, total happiness in your job is almost a right—anything else is letting yourself down and living less than a whole life. He is not alone in that perception; it is pervasive.

This is tricky to understand because work is good; it's one of the things we were placed on this earth to do—we should value work and even enjoy it. But it seems that our desires have been skewed.

Today our dreams around work are rooted in many of the same desires as those of previous generations—security, comfort, accomplishment, expression, individuality—but with two significant differences: our dreams tend to be simultaneously more grandiose and more self-centered. As we look outward, we dream of changing the world, making a difference, and leaving our mark. As we look inward, we dream of loving ourselves, being whole, and achieving self-actualization. So we look for a job that will help us fulfill both the grand outward dreams and the self-focused ones (or rather, we look to fulfill the self through outward accomplishments).

We want a satisfying job, but we often define satisfaction differently than previous generations did. No longer is financial security enough. We measure satisfaction more by the emotions than the biweekly paycheck or company pension plan. The question we ask of our job is: do I *feel* satisfied?

Don't believe me? Think about how often people change careers now compared to previous generations. Consider the number of professional athletes who want to be musicians, the number of musicians who want to be actors, and the number of actors who want to run for political office.

Or think about the number of times you've heard someone talk wistfully about branching out on their own, being their own boss, and earning a living through doing what they are passionate about. Entrepreneurialism is often seen as the peak of vocational success and as the panacea for workplace dissatisfaction. It is fast-moving, challenging, and fulfilling; and ideally it makes a difference in the world too. It's basically a workplace utopia—financial success blended with total freedom and a dose of goodwill toward mankind.

Or how many people do you know who dream about doing something creative for a living? Books, poetry, music, visual arts, screenplays, drama, dance—these are certainly all good things. It would be great to create something meaningful and beautiful, and gain critical acclaim and commercial success at the same time.

Whether it's entrepreneurial or artistic, most of us dream of doing work that matters and of having the freedom to do so on our own terms. We want the work to be quality, and we want it to connect with the right people. We want to be in charge of the schedule, the direction, and the purpose. Of course, we still want to make a living (and there will be many people reading this for whom just getting by is a big enough dream in itself). But most of us want more than work that pays; we want work that we love.

TODAY'S DREAMS: RELATIONAL FULFILLMENT

The second defining dream of Western culture is the desire for relational fulfillment. We yearn for it, imagine it, and fantasize about it. The cultural atmosphere in which we live both subtly and explicitly tells us—through advertising, music, movies, television, books, podcasts, and just about any other medium—that wholeness and happiness come through a meaningful relationship. If we don't have such a relationship, we need to find one. And if we do have such a relationship, we picture all the ways in which it could be better.

When we read the word "relationship," we instinctively read it as referring to a *romantic* relationship; and when we think of romantic relationships, we usually think of *sexual* relationships. In most people's minds, it is inconceivable that a person could be happy without the freedom to have sexual relationships of whatever quality and quantity they desire.

This is too often true among Christians as well. Many of us have come to believe what society tells us about which relationships are most meaningful and which ones offer true happiness. Romantic sexual relationships are ultimate; other types of relationship are, if not second tier, then somehow diminished; and relationships that aren't fulfilling need to be ended quickly. This isn't to say that we care nothing about meaningful friendships (that would make us a sociopath). It's that the subconscious sexualization of our minds has shaped how we think happiness can be found.

Our skewed beliefs are actually based in truth. (After all, the best lies include a healthy dose of truth, or they would never be believed.) We are relational beings. God made us to be in community: to have deep friendships and with the capacity to fall in love. The gravitational pull we feel toward relational intimacy is God-given. Yet instead of looking for happiness in the plethora of relationships God created (sibling, cousin, friend, parent, neighbor, co-worker, significant other, etc.), we've limited the promise of deepest happiness to one kind of relationship. By putting all our chips on that square we have more chance of going broke than winning the happiness jackpot.

SO... HOW'S EVERYBODY DOING?

So after decades of dedicated pursuit of these dreams... How are we? Are we happy? Have we arrived at a fulfilled dream?

According to my observation and experience, the answers to these questions are, in order: not well, nope, and not yet and with little hope of ever doing so. We are stressed and anxious and dissatisfied. The grander our dreams get and the more they turn inward, the less happy we seem to be. Our response to this unhappiness is to pursue our dream harder or to pursue another version of the same dream—another job, another cause, another relationship. If the definition of insanity is trying the same thing repeatedly and expecting different results, well, we have just diagnosed ourselves.

Which raises the question: why in the world do we keep doing this to ourselves?

THE WISH YOUR HEART MAKES

Cinderella has crooned these seminal words to tens of millions of people over the years: "A dream is a wish your heart makes … If you keep on believing, the dream that you wish will come true." These lyrics encapsulate the direction we feel we must take in order to find happiness: we must follow our hearts! Listen to your heart's desires, conjure a dream, and then get after it.

But if chasing dreams leads only to more chasing, and if our dreams are not delivering on their promise of satisfaction, how reliable are our hearts really? Think about it.

When we don't have something, our hearts want it.

When we have plenty of something, plenty is never enough. Our hearts want more.

When someone else has something, our hearts want what they have.

When we have a hundred different things, our hearts want the hundred and first thing.

When we have accomplished something, our hearts immediately turn to somewhere else where we might succeed.

Our hearts always want something more, newer, better, different—whether it be in regard to sex, money, achievement, self-esteem, health, fitness, attractiveness, job satisfaction, relational fulfillment, purpose, or anything. So our hearts make wishes which become our dreams, and then we chase. And we chase. And we chase some more. And yet our hearts are not satisfied.

Our dreams don't ever come fully or lastingly true. The job is stimulating and you post on Instagram about how it's your "dream job," for about six weeks. You train for the half marathon and feel amazing; then you finish the race. You get married, and it's blissful; then conflict happens and trust issues arise. I could go on, but you've lived this in one way or a hundred and know full well what I am writing about—if, that is, you're willing to pause in the midst of the chase and reflect on it for a moment.

A KIND OF HAPPINESS

Now for a necessary clarification: I don't think life is bad. Nor do I think meaningful work, money, achievements, creative ventures, relationships, or sex are bad. God didn't put us in this world to be miserable. Quite the opposite—the world is overflowing with good things, pleasurable things, things that deliver happiness. And they are created by God. He intended us for happiness.

And sometimes we *are* happy. If our pursuit of happiness turned up nothing at all, life would be bleaker than a Cormac McCarthy novel and sadder than a Jason Isbell song. The reason we keep chasing our dreams is because they do deliver a version of happiness, at least for a time and to an extent. Having money and possessions is nice. Accomplishing things is satisfying. Getting fit feels great and looks good. Sex is enjoyable. These things make us happy.

But we have gotten happiness twisted. We cannot escape the words of the Old Testament prophet Jeremiah: "The heart is deceitful above all things, and desperately sick" (Jeremiah 17:9). Dreams are the wishes our hearts make, but our hearts are not reliable guides. Our hearts have taken good things from God and conjured up fever dreams of them as things in which we can find our identity and on which we can build our lives. But these objects of happiness were not created to bear that burden.

As one man in Scripture knew better than most...

ALL IS VANITY

No book in the Bible speaks to a life of chasing dreams and trying to be happy like Ecclesiastes. And, boy, does it start with a bang. After a phrase of introduction these are the first words from the mouth of the Preacher:

Vanity of vanities, says the Preacher,
   vanity of vanities! All is vanity. (Ecclesiastes 1:1-2)

From this point, Solomon (the Preacher)—the wealthiest king of his day and the wisest man in history (non-Jesus division)—obliterates the things on which we place our expectations of happiness category by category. He starts with a sweeping statement and backs it up throughout the remainder of this chapter and the entire book. We will come back to Ecclesiastes often as a foundation for understanding happiness, expectations, and reality in general. For now, though, focus on this core statement: all is, in fact, vanity.

What does that mean? To understand the remainder of the passage, and the rest of the book, understanding this word is vital. Today we talk about "vanity" as being proud in one's appearance. We think of it as something shallow and inherently valueless.

That isn't what the Preacher in Ecclesiastes means, though. David Gibson, in his excellent book *Living Life Backward*, explains it this way: "The Preacher is saying that everything is a mist, a vapor, a puff of wind, a bit of smoke" (Crossway 2017, p 19). His use of vanity means ephemeral, passing, vaporous. He is saying that everything in this life has limits to its value because it has limits to its life span. The implication is that "all is vanity" *if we try to find permanent satisfaction and happiness in it.* The point is the *temporal* nature of the happiness we find in this life, not that there is no happiness to be found in life.

Temporal does not mean sinful or foolish or idolatrous. It just means temporary. So Ecclesiastes is not saying that happiness is pointless. It is saying that seeking lasting happiness and basing our hopes on temporal things is sinful, foolish, and idolatrous. Ecclesiastes reframes our understanding of happiness in terms of time, eternity, and mortality. And that reframing must reframe our dreams and how we chase them.

IT'S NOT ALL BAD NEWS

The goal of this book is not to ruin your happiness. It is not to bring a storm cloud into every sunny day, point out every looming disappointment, predict the failure at the end of every success, and revel in the inevitable disappointments of life. I hate unhappiness. I hate yours and mine.

My aim in this book is to help you discover a happiness that is better than that which your dreams have promised you. It is to reframe your expectations in a way that reflects reality as God defines it in the Bible, so that they are true. It is to set you free from the manic pursuit, so that you can live a life that's grounded, hopeful, and, yes, genuinely happy.

CHAPTER 2

EXPECTING
JUST RIGHT

When I was in college there was a girl I really liked. We'd gone to dinner or had coffee together a couple of times, but it was hardly what you could call dating. I wanted to figure out how to change that. A good friend, always the reliable wingman, suggested we take this girl and her roommate on a double date to a concert by the pop country band Rascal Flatts. Surely a short road trip to a fun concert of pop love songs would be just the spark to kindle our relationship. We asked them, and they jumped at the chance.

The concert was a ninety-minute drive away, so we laid out a casual but detailed itinerary for dinner, the drive, and then the concert. Dinner was lovely, and the drive was going swimmingly as we flew west on I-80 across Illinois, cranking out the tunes of the band we were heading to see.

This was when I started to get the sense that something might not be shaping up quite right. For some reason it only dawned on me then that I hated every song we were listening to. The band was terrible. To compound this auditory disaster, both girls *adored* them.

My bad mood soured the vibe, and the evening went

downhill from there—with minimal eye contact and even less conversation. On the way home I was loudly silent while the other three gushed about how great the concert was, and then the girls fell asleep. All my hoping, planning, and best efforts led to barely a wave goodbye. Not only was there no spark; there was a torrential downpour to wash my hopes away. Needless to say, it was a disappointing evening.

PLANNING FOR HAPPINESS

As my double-date disaster illustrates, we spend vast amounts of energy making plans and arranging our lives with this one goal in mind: to get maximum happiness. Most of what we do has a direct line of sight to a happy outcome: we eat for pleasure, joke for laughter, converse for friendship, sleep for rest, and so on. It is pretty easy to explain how what we do should result in a happier existence.

Not that we only ever do things that offer immediate happiness—that would be insane. So much of maturity is learning the value of delayed gratification: realizing that greater happiness can be had by waiting and persevering. So we do painful things for the sake of happiness, like working out. We do challenging things for the sake of happiness, like going to therapy for our mental health. We persevere through miserable circumstances in the belief that the way *to* happiness is *through* and that we'll find it on the other side.

So in much of life, there is a gap in time between the actions we take in pursuit of happiness and the result we anticipate. This gap is filled with waiting. More specifically, it is filled with our *expectations*. Sometimes our expectations are clear and stated—we want good results that will make us feel happy. Most often, though, our expectations reside below the surface of conscious thought. When we take action—any action—it is with the gut-level expectation that happiness will result eventually. But what if it doesn't?

WITH EXPECTATION COMES...

Every action is tied to an expectation. Every disappointment is an unmet expectation. So then, every action can lead to disappointment.

In case you skimmed that, let me repeat: *every disappointment is an unmet expectation.*

While a hope is something you would *like* to see happen, an expectation is a graduated hope—one that has moved from being wished to being counted on. For example, I am a fan of the Minnesota Vikings. Every year I hope they will win the Super Bowl, but over the years I have learned not to *expect* it. When you say, "I'm trying not to get my hopes up"—about an audition call back, a job interview, or a date—you *already* have your hopes up, in the sense that you *want* it to happen. But it's not your hopes you're trying to keep in check; it's your expectations. Negative outcomes hurt because we wish they were different. But the pain is magnified a thousandfold by *expecting* the outcome to be different.

Our foiled plans are disappointing because we expect them to work. Any parent can remember a time or eleven when they made plans with their kids to do something fun—fishing together, camping, getting ice cream, going to a ballgame, seeing a movie—and things started to go sideways. The kids decide to whine and fight, it rains, the mosquitoes swarm, or the movie is sold out. We're disappointed because we expected our plans to make everyone happy, but they didn't. If we'd anticipated the possibility of things going badly, we'd actually have had an easier time shrugging off the frustration.

IS IT BETTER TO EXPECT NOTHING?

So if expectations lead so consistently to disappointment, wouldn't it be better to do without them—to expect nothing? This seems like the logical, if cynical, next question.

The answer is a definitive NO.

For one thing, we're not able to expect nothing. To envision a future, to anticipate anything, to make a plan, or to set a goal inevitably involves expectation. It may be vague, suppressed, or unexpressed—but it is an expectation. An attempt to eliminate these would be fruitless at best and insanity at worst because it would mean avoiding all thoughts of the future.

And it wouldn't make us happy. It would leave us feeling aimless because what is the point of making a plan if you expect no results? It would leave us feeling lonely because what would be the point of investing in relationships if we expected no intimacy? To say, "I expect nothing and hope for nothing out of life" would leave little reason to live at all. It would drain meaning and goodness from any experience.

If eliminating expectations is impossible (and a terrible idea), might it be more effective to simply *lower* our expectations?

Again, the answer is no.

True, decreasing our expectations will, in one sense, decrease our disappointment. But it will not increase our happiness overall. If anything, it will simply leave us with a more generalized disappointment. Lowering expectations across the board means we'll forgo opportunities for significant satisfaction. To live a life with small expectations is to live a life with small joys and little gladness. Expectations set us up for disappointment, sure, but they give us motivation and direction too. We may be able avoid particular disappointments by lowering our expectations, but this isn't the path to happiness either.

WHAT GOLDILOCKS GOT RIGHT

So what *should* we do with our expectations? We need to look no further than the story of Goldilocks and the three bears.

In this timeless children's tale, a carefree little girl stumbles upon a house in the woods while its occupants, three bears, are away. Being curious, and obnoxiously nosy, she decides to have a look around.

In the living room she tests out their chairs and finds one to be too small, one to be too large, and the third to be just right. Then she gets hungry and makes her way to the kitchen, where she finds three bowls of porridge (a word to make oatmeal sound less nasty). The first is too cold, the second is too hot, but the third is just right. After all her exploring and snacking, Goldilocks is getting sleepy so off she goes to find a place to nap. In the bedroom she tests one bed and finds it too soft, and the second bed she finds too hard, but the third is just right. We'll leave the story here because there is some debate as to whether, when the bears get home, they eat Goldilocks or she escapes having learned a valuable lesson about snooping and personal property.

What has this fable to do with the pursuit of happiness? Our instinct is to expect too much. Our defense mechanism is to expect too little. What we need is the option that is *just right*. It does exist, and we can find it (without breaking and entering).

As we seek to find right expectations, we need to understand where our expectations go wrong. The problem is not simply that we expect *too much* or *too little*. It is not just a matter of quantity—how *much* we expect—but what we expect too much *of*.

Sometimes we place our expectations on *wrong things*, like when we expect any happiness to be delivered by things that are sinful. Take, for example, pornography, gossip, workaholism, and greed. We might look to them to deliver happiness, but we will always be left disappointed. Yes, sin stimulates senses and offers immediate pleasure, but it eventually leaves us feeling diminished as people and further from God. Consider your own heart, desires, and motivations for a moment. What aspects of your life you are counting on for happiness that are against God's expressed will?

Other times we place *wrong expectations on right things*. This is when we expect things to deliver one kind of happiness, when God actually designed them to give us a different aspect of happiness. So, for example, we look to significant others for spiritual fulfillment. We look to friends to make us feel whole. We look to food and drink to ease anxiety or depression. God gave us these and so many other wonderful gifts to make us happy—profoundly happy—but when we demand of them things God did not intend, we are left empty. This is a subtle, quiet misplacement of expectations that so often starts out right but then goes wrong. So we must consider what good things in our lives have taken too high a place. What, if we lost it, would make us enraged at God? What do we instinctively turn to when we need to numb the pain?

The real crux of our problem is that we expect *temporal things* to deliver *lasting happiness*. The issue is not that we expect *any* happiness from temporal things—God created countless wonderful things, people, places, and experiences to give us genuine happiness. It is that we expect *lasting* happiness from these things. Even the good things God gives us will not last forever; everything has a life span—everything decays. No created thing can fill the void in our lives forever, or even for long.

When we consider how this looks in our lives, it can be scary because it is tangential to death. Are we so afraid of the reality of our own death that we refuse to face it in other circumstances: the death of a pet, a car, or a career? If so, we have inflated our expectations of what those things can offer us beyond what God intended.

Finally, we can even expect too much of God. Or rather we expect too much *of the wrong* things from God—things he never promised to do or give or be. We expect him to work in our preferred time frame. We expect him to give us whatever we ask for. We expect him to be merciful but not wrathful. We expect him to keep us from all difficulty and pain and trial. We expect him to reveal the mysterious and the confusing. Then we find ourselves disappointed when he fails to deliver on our expectations, as if he is beholden to us.

Goldilocks understood something that we often miss: happiness is found in the sweet spot between too much and too little. Happiness is found in expecting the right things of the right things. She tried the extremes but found contentment in the third option. So must we.

"JUST RIGHT" EXPECTATIONS

It's not easy to take a step back and examine our motivations like this. But it is necessary. It's how we know whether we are living for the right things, hoping for the right things, and expecting the right things. And it's why Ecclesiastes is in the Bible, to sort out our priorities in big, blunt sweeps.

Ecclesiastes 3:10-15 says:

I have seen the business that God has given to the children of man to be busy with. He has made everything beautiful in its time. Also, he has put eternity into man's heart, yet so that he cannot find out what God has done from the beginning to the end. I perceived that there is nothing better for them than to be joyful and to do good as long as they live; also that everyone should eat and drink and take pleasure in all his toil—this is God's gift to man.

I perceived that whatever God does endures forever; nothing can be added to it, nor anything taken from it. God has done it, so that people fear before him. That which is, already has been; that which is to be, already has been; and God seeks what has been driven away.

This passage shows us that everything is beautiful *in its time*, but not everything is beautiful forever. Not everything is meant to give lasting happiness. Rather, temporal things are meant to point toward eternal happiness. We enjoy them richly now, because they are good, while also seeking to "set [our] minds on things that are above, not on things that are on earth" (Colossians 3:2).

Yet it's no surprise that we want things to last. Ecclesiastes 3:11 says that God has "put eternity into man's heart." We are made for eternity: gravitationally pulled toward things that last—things of God. That is where our truest and lasting happiness is meant to come from, and it is why we so often have immense expectations; everyone, whether they believe in God or not, has a deep internal yearning for eternal significance and happiness.

At the same time, we are unable to understand the infinity of God (v 11b). Because we are finite beings confined to an earthly life span and limited knowledge, we seek the entirety of our happiness in things we can wrap our minds around— things that are readily available. We struggle to trust that God really will deliver a happiness that's beyond the scope of our imaginations on the other side of the grave. So we place the weight of eternity on temporal things and end up disappointed.

"Just right" expectations live in the tension of finding real happiness in temporal things while knowing that they are not forever. "Just right" expectations look ahead to eternity for eternal happiness for God's people, but are also grounded in this life and the experiences that it offers.

How do we stay grounded in this life? Verses 12-13 tells us: there is "nothing better" for us than to "be joyful and to do good" as long as we live and to "eat and drink and take pleasure" in our toil. Life is not drudgery, not void of meaning, not void of happiness. There is joy to be found in doing good and in resting our expectations on good things. Having eternity in our hearts and looking ahead to the happiness of heaven does not remove the meaning or joy from this life. There is God-given pleasure in food and drink. There is God-given satisfaction in the fruit of our work. This is our lot in these few decades on earth, and it is a good lot. An eternal perspective gives us healthy expectations for temporal things, because it makes us value them for what they are intended to be.

What God does "endures forever" without addition or subtraction, and he acts "so that people fear before him" (v 14). This is our ultimate defining reality. This means we are to worship him in awe, submit to his perfect authority, rest in his immeasurable strength, and know the extent of his mercy and judgment. We are not our own deity. We do not determine what is good or bad. Our happiness and future are in his hands. Our best is defined by his will and plan, and we can be at peace knowing that God does want our best.

Goldilocks found her "just right" in the middle—not too hot or cold or hard or soft or tall or short. In one sense our "just right" is in the middle too, holding in tension right expectations for temporal things in this life and looking ahead to eternal happiness with God. The difference is that we are not finding a way between two extremes, but rather finding the right sort of happiness now *and* a right anticipation for the eternal.

"Just right" expectations are those that rest in godly realism. They put the things of earth—work, family, romantic love, food and drink, friendship—in their proper place and do so without diminishing their good. In fact, we rightly relish the good *only* when our expectations are rightly oriented. In this way, "just right" expectations free us to enjoy and move us to worship, as we grow in understanding of the eternal immensity of God, our Creator and Giver.

CHAPTER 3

HANGING HAPPINESS ON WEAK HOOKS

Every Christmas during my childhood, a member of our church who worked at an office-supply company would give my family a massive gift bag—think Santa's toy sack—of office and home supplies. While not the most festive gift to give the pastor's family, it was significantly more useful than the ties my dad received or the fruit cakes that got dropped off. It was overflowing with lint rollers, packing tape, sticky notes, ball point pens, highlighters, and more. Like any gift assortment (or candy assortment, or fruit tray), certain things filtered to the bottom and were the last to be claimed. In this bag, those were the adhesive-backed plastic hanging hooks.

It was only once I moved out and became responsible for my own home that I began to covet them. They seemed ideal for hanging pictures or dust mops or calendars... until I actually tried them.

I would position the hook just so, gingerly place the picture frame on it, and step back to judge if it was level. Satisfied,

I'd go on with life until an hour or a day or a week later when I'd be startled out of my skin by a loud crash. Once my heart rate had slowed and I determined that there wasn't a burglar or poltergeist, I'd find the frame twisted and broken with the hook lying nearby, completely detached from the wall. It simply wasn't strong enough to hold the weight. And yet, for some reason, I'd just grab another hook and try again.

PREDICTABLE RESULTS

We hang happiness on hooks in the same way that I hung pictures, thinking that our job or our kids or our vacation can bear the weight of our expectation. The problem, though, is that our expectations for happiness are too heavy for the hooks we use. Those little plastic ones are designed for light or temporary weights, but we weigh them down with expectations for deep and lasting happiness.

I was slow to learn my lesson, but eventually I figured out what kinds of hooks I needed for heavier pictures. We are much slower to learn what kinds of hooks we can hang heavy expectations on. We keep being shocked when they crash into pieces on the floor. Then we grab the same kind of hook, maybe in a different color this time, and try again with predictably disappointing results. Next we try moving the hook to a different location. Same results. And we just keep on going, rarely, if ever, considering whether our hooks are strong enough to support the happiness we expect.

So what are the some of the weak hooks that we might be expecting too much from?

WORK

It's always exciting when you see an announcement on social media of someone starting a new job. For the first few weeks they'll post regularly about how thrilled they are about this "new adventure" and how great their co-workers are, sharing pictures from the new office. Then, over the next few weeks, the posts will slow to a trickle and then dry up completely. This is what I like to call the "Expense Report Pivot"—the moment when reality has set in and they realize that this "dream job" involves some level of drudgery too. The day-to-day reality of what they hoped would change their lives turns out not to be all that glamorous or exciting. The hook of a new job could not hold the weight of their hopes for it. So before long, they search for another hook just like the last one but in a different place.

Most of us quietly believe that work can support the weight of our happiness. It's a belief encapsulated by that guy who told me, "Man, if you don't *love* your job, you should quit and go find something else." All we have to do is keep looking for that perfect job, the one we just love, that truly grand adventure. It is a seductively believable attitude. If only it was true.

Switching jobs is not sin; it can be good and necessary. Sometimes a work situation is untenable because of poor fit, poor leadership, unethical practices, or the like. Sometimes we need to find a new job because we cannot support ourselves or our family financially. Sometimes God makes it clear that we should pursue something new (as he did to me about two years after that conversation). None of these reasons are based in "I just don't love it." None of them are seeking to move our happiness from one weak hook to another.

Work is a good hook for the right expectations. We were created by God to be workers. In Genesis 1 and 2 God gave mankind "dominion" over the earth. He gave Adam a garden to cultivate and the task of naming every animal. From the very beginning work has been part of our purpose, and at its best, work does make us happy because it allows us to exercise our talents, use our creativity, partner with other people, do something beneficial for others, and find a measure of fulfillment.

But work cannot fulfill our dreams or make us lastingly happy: "Whatever your hand finds to do, do it with your might, for there is no work or thought or knowledge or wisdom in Sheol, to which you are going" (Ecclesiastes 9:10). We work hard now, and our work matters in this life. We work for the good of family, society, and self but not to find eternal meaning or identity. When we seek that kind of happiness and significance in work, we are hanging our expectations on a weak hook.

LOVE AND MARRIAGE

I got married at twenty-two on a warm May day with friends and family there to celebrate. On that day I had the highest hopes and happiest dreams. We had a whole life ahead of us. Sure, we would face challenges, but what were those in the face of love and youth and confidence?

Eleven and a half years later my phone rang as I drove across snowy Wisconsin, and I was informed that the divorce had been finalized. All those hopes and dreams had wafted away with barely a whisper.

I went into marriage expecting my wife to be what she could not be, and she did the same toward me. And both of us believed ourselves capable of giving the other happiness; we subconsciously believed the lie of "you are my everything." We both would have professed to putting God first and finding our identity in him, but neither of us could have told you precisely what that meant or how to do it. I thought she completed me, and she thought I was a paragon of virtuous manhood. And we set about disappointing each other's expectations.

Rather than leave me jaded toward marriage or skeptical of love, though, my failed marriage opened my eyes to the purity and beauty and miracle of genuine love between a husband and wife. The soul-wrenching pain I experienced set in stark relief the magnificence of what marriage *can* and *should* be.

A good marriage is miraculous because our tendency is not to give ourselves to others but to take from them, need from them, demand of them. Yet love is of God, and he has shared it with his image-bearers. A truly good marriage should surprise us in the best way, because it's always far more than two sinners deserve or can construct on their own. Marital bliss is not automatic. We expect our relationship to be mostly easy, mostly natural; yet in all marriages—even the best marriages—it takes work.

It is so easy to expect that love from another, or the chance to love another, will solve our woes and fill our voids. In our Western society, marriage is almost universally viewed as a means to personal happiness through companionship, sex, and love (but not necessarily sacrificial, costly love).

When we view marriage this way, we have created a hook too weak to support the hopes of happiness we place on it. As with work, marriage is a good hook for the right expectations. But a self-seeking and self-fulfilling perspective on marriage *is* a weak hook. Love is not a weak hook, but a version of love centered on feelings more than commitment, getting rather than giving, and being filled rather than pouring into another is. When we try to hang our happiness on these warped versions of beautiful, God-given things, it inevitably leads to disappointment, frustration, and pain.

FRIENDSHIP

I moved from the Chicago area to Nashville when I was thirty years old. I had lived in Chicago since college and so had a web of friendships that had been years in the making. Then I up and left it all.

After I had unpacked the boxes, figured out how to get to the office, and I was able to navigate to the grocery store without using GPS, I realized *I had no friends in Tennessee.* I had no history with anyone. I had no shared stories or inside jokes. I had nobody I could lean on or trust or celebrate with. And I had no real idea how to make a friend. It seemed weird and creepy to start asking folks, "Will you be my friend?" I knew I needed them, but I hadn't put much thought into what makes true friendships and what to expect from them. I suspect that few of us have.

This lack of thought means that it's very easy to bring unhealthy expectations and hopes to friendship. Maybe we become jealous when our friend befriends someone else and spends time with them. This kind of jealousy reveals an expectation of exclusivity or primacy and is born from a place of insecurity and selfishness. It shows that we are in this friendship mainly for the sake of our own fulfillment and security, not out of love for the other. If we can't exhibit any joy on the other's behalf or selflessly want their best, that should be a warning sign to us.

It's also possible for a kind of co-dependence to develop between "best friends." Close friendships can be rich, deep, and life-giving. But they can also become in-grown, and we can over-invest in them at the expense of other relationships. If one person has become "my person," it might be that I am leaning too heavily on them for emotional support and life input. And that can leave adjacent friends feeling just that— adjacent rather than connected.

When it comes to making new friends, most of us expect it to just work—we want to "click." Yet in almost any developing friendship we'll experience an awkwardness when we're unfamiliar with each other. And as we get closer, we'll encounter the awkwardness of exposure. It feels vulnerable and risky. How will they respond to us the more they get to know the *real* us? While some people connect more quickly than others, the reality is that most genuine friendships have to work through the awkward, vulnerable, and difficult parts before they get to that place of easy peace and comfort.

Friendship isn't easy. Consider Jesus, the only perfect man who ever lived and history's greatest friend. He spent three years pouring himself into twelve men, three of whom (Peter, James, and John) were especially close to him. They shared life, home, and ministry. Yet when Jesus faced a bogus trial built on trumped-up charges brought by petty and jealous officials, his closest friends abandoned and denied him. One betrayed him. If even the perfect Son of God experienced these sorts of fractured relationships through no sin of his own, it gives us all the more reason to pay careful attention to what we are seeking from our friendships, where sinners are involved on both sides. It is too easy to expect too much of the wrong things from friendships and then find our happiness in pieces when the weak hook breaks.

CHURCH

Few of us would say we are looking for the perfect church. We know it doesn't exist. Instead we look for a church that is perfect *for us*. We want an environment that feels comfortable, music we like, preaching that connects with us, small groups where we feel at home, ministries to serve our needs and where we can exercise our gifts, and leadership that is wise and humble and godly and perpetually available. None of these wishes are wrong in themselves. It is possible to have reasonable expectations of a church and still be let down by other people's sin (and what I have in mind here is certainly not in the category of bullying or spiritual abuse). Yet in many cases our expectations are too high; few churches excel across all areas of ministry, and even fewer do so while connecting with a wide variety of people. For most churches, excelling in one area means necessarily de-emphasizing something else, so there are always going to be weaknesses.

When the hook breaks and our church disappoints us, it hurts. But our response is not usually very good. We are prone to grumbling and sharing with anyone who will listen about what we wish was different, exacerbating the issue rather than resolving it. Instead of self-examination and a willingness to contribute to change, we put the burden on others, creating greater conflict and spreading unhappiness.

Often we hang back, withholding participation or attendance. Sometimes this is from pain, but more frequently it's just sulking. Perhaps we pick up the pieces from the floor and go elsewhere to hang them on a different church's hook.

So what are the right expectations to have of church? So long as we approach church primarily as a service provider, it will leave us disappointed. Instead, we should view it in the way Scripture depicts it: as a family and as a body. It is always quirky, often dysfunctional, sometimes aggravating, and occasionally confusing, and it always takes work and care to make it healthy. We are right to depend on it, but we should also know its flaws and weaknesses. Our preferences and needs are insatiable and constantly changing, so no church will be able to meet them for long. To view the church as a service to me is to make it into a weak hook; to love the church as our body is to make it into a good hook.

SELF

Sometimes we realize that even our expectations for ourselves haven't been fulfilled. I have several vivid mental snapshots of moments when I've thought, "This isn't where I pictured myself."

Two years into marriage, carrying a diaper bag in one hand, a Hello Kitty backpack stuffed with dolls over my shoulder, and my firstborn daughter in my other arm. I did not picture myself as a dad in my early twenties, especially not the dad to a daughter. I loved it, but I was playing catch up.

Climbing on the scale one day at age 25 to realize I was 40 pounds (18kg) heavier than when I finished college.

Replacing countless hours of intramural sports with a desk job and a soft-drink addiction will do that. I never pictured myself becoming the dad who needs to diet and exercise, but there I was.

Being summoned to the conference room of my company at age 26 to be informed I was being fired. I earned my way out the door. I deserved it. But I had never pictured myself as unemployed, trying to explain to friends and family what had happened, seeking to regain trust, and trying to support a family.

Turning 30 and still living in the Chicago suburbs. I had tried to find an opportunity to move away a dozen times to no avail. I felt stagnant.

The phone call at age 33 when my wife said it was over between us as I paced the hall of our apartment, four steps up and four steps back, like a caged animal. I had pictured a lot of things: buying a home, seeing our kids graduate college, figuring out how to pay for weddings for two daughters, maybe grandkids, sitting in a rocking chair on the porch together sipping coffee. But I never pictured the blank future I was faced with then.

In other cases, our unmet expectations for ourselves have more to do with the kinds of people we are rather than the circumstances of our lives. We are dissatisfied with our body type, our shyness, our Enneagram number, our habits, our work ethic, or our spiritual lives. We have character traits we wish we could change: argumentativeness, ego, laziness, being overly opinionated, being critical. (Ok, that's me, but I'm sure you have your own.) We picture ourselves as someone else, someone *better*.

Every day we wish we could change something, or a thousand things, about our lives. Every day we disappoint ourselves. And every night we have to lie down and go to sleep, knowing we have not lived up to our own expectations.

We are not strong enough hooks to hold the weight of our own happiness. Not in our own strength, at least. As in every other example of misplaced hope, the expectations we put on ourselves are often born out of what we think is best, not what God has said is best. They're defined by our best effort at wisdom rather than resting in his perfect wisdom. But they don't have to be.

WHAT IS WRONG?

Each of the categories we've considered—work, marriage, friendship, church, and self, as well as so many others—is a means of finding happiness. They are designed by God and are good things. They are good hooks for the right things, but they are too weak to hold our hopes for total happiness. So take a look back through each of those categories. Can you think of a time when you experienced the hook breaking? What weighty expectations were you placing on it? What other weak hooks are you relying on for happiness?

It's incumbent on us to be aware of our expectations and gauge whether they align with reality and what is true according to God. We can only do this when we realize another thing: all the hooks are broken. In the next chapter we'll explore why this is. But thankfully, this is not the whole story. We are not doomed to repeat this cycle of shattered hopes and broken happiness. There *is* a way to get expectations right and find strong hooks on which to hang them—there *is* a way to be happy.

CHAPTER 4

WE LIVE
CURSED

So far this book sort of resembles cable news television: a bunch of channels with nothing but bad news. You should be fairly convinced by now that life is neither how we'd like it to be nor how it's supposed to be. So now we're confronted with the question of "Why is life like this?"

Because it's cursed.

When I hear the word "curse," the phrases that come to mind are from great stories (e.g. "always winter and never Christmas" from *The Lion, the Witch, and the Wardrobe* or "Avada Kedavra," the killing curse from the Harry Potter books) or from baseball's superstitions (e.g. the Curse of the Billy Goat or the Curse of the Bambino, which hung over the Chicago Cubs and the Boston Red Sox for decades). A curse is a plot device, a superstition, an unfortunate set of circumstances without a clear explanation—nothing more.

Scripture depicts a curse as something altogether different. We're introduced to a curse, or rather the curse, near the very beginning. Genesis 1 and 2 tell the story of God making the world, creating humanity as his sinless image-bearers, and commissioning them as his caretakers of Earth. When God looked upon his creation, he declared it good; it was right and perfect, as he intended. He placed Adam and Eve in a garden where they were free to eat and live and enjoy this paradise and their union in perfect harmony. God walked with them, and they were unafraid and unashamed because all was right.

Then comes Genesis 3. With just a little prompting and a few well-placed lies from Satan, they were persuaded that they could attain God-like knowledge and power, and that God's warning, that they would die as a consequence, was false. They took authority into their own hands and ate from the one tree in the garden that God had forbidden, and all hell broke loose, quite literally. Their actions were what is called "the fall," when mankind stepped from sinless perfection and union with God into rebellion and brokenness.

God's right and just response to this rebellion was the curse. This was no wand-waving spell or needle in a voodoo doll, as if God were wielding evil. Nor was God playing the part of seer and merely predicting a curse that would come. No—the curse was, and is, God's intentional, fair, and just response to mankind's rejection of the infinite, perfect, and good God. The curse is the judgment of God wielded with sovereign power, not some runaway evil rampaging through the world. And it encapsulates every part of life:

> *The LORD God said to the serpent,*
> *"Because you have done this,*
> *cursed are you above all livestock*
> *and above all beasts of the field;*
> *on your belly you shall go,*
> *and dust you shall eat*
> *all the days of your life.*
> *I will put enmity between you and the woman,*
> *and between your offspring and her offspring;*
> *he shall bruise your head,*
> *and you shall bruise his heel."*

To the woman he said,
"I will surely multiply your pain in childbearing;
*   in pain you shall bring forth children.*
Your desire shall be contrary to your husband,
*   but he shall rule over you."*

And to Adam he said,
"Because you have listened to the voice of your wife
*   and have eaten of the tree*
of which I commanded you,
*   'You shall not eat of it,'*
cursed is the ground because of you;
*   in pain you shall eat of it all the days of your life;*
thorns and thistles it shall bring forth for you;
*   and you shall eat the plants of the field.*
By the sweat of your face
*   you shall eat bread,*
till you return to the ground,
*   for out of it you were taken;*
for you are dust,
*   and to dust you shall return." (Genesis 3:14-19)*

THE CURSE'S CONTEXT

Moments before these words were uttered, all had been well in the world—*all* had been well.

We can scarcely imagine a world like this. Yes, we can imagine good days and beautiful places and delightful moments and deep love and sublime harmonies and blue skies. But even the richest, happiest moments for us are interspersed with drudgery, pain, frustration, sadness, and loss. We never have untainted happiness.

Yet that's what existed in Eden: perfect peace and harmony between all living things. Everything doing precisely what it was created to do. So Adam and Eve did not tip the scales from pretty decent to pretty bad but rather from perfect to cursed.

If we struggle to comprehend the scale of the punishment, it's probably because we underestimate the nature of the crime. God's holiness is his infinite perfection in all things and the very essence of his being as *God*. It is what sets him apart from all created things. When Adam and Eve disobeyed God, they were not just breaking rules or disrespecting authority. They were spitting upon the infinity of God's goodness. When finite, created beings attempt to usurp the throne of the infinitely holy Creator, the consequences are dire.

THE CURSE'S REACH

The cost of rebellion against God was a move from perfect rightness in everything to wrongness in everything. That's not to say that everything is as wrong as it could be, for that would be hell. But it is to say that there is not one untainted moment or item or person or idea or thought or feeling or inanimate object in the entire universe.

More than that, the curse brought death into the world. The leap from life to death sounds insignificant when put in words on a page. But anyone who has experienced a loss knows that the chasm between life and death is immeasurable. In life a person breathes and hums and expresses themselves with energy. They relate and interact and feel. They are a *person*. In death, in a moment, a person becomes a husk, a physical remnant of what once was a whole life. And the curse was a move from life to death for all things everywhere. Death has defined the limits of everything since.

If you listed the specific parts of life that are cursed in Genesis 3 it would be a short list: pain in childbearing, marital conflict, difficulty and fruitlessness in work, mortality. The curse is not a comprehensive list of life experiences. Rather it is comprehensive in category.

First, and above all, it is a spiritual curse. After Adam and Eve sinned, "the eyes of both were opened, and they knew that they were naked" (3:7) and they hid themselves from God. They knew guilt and shame for the first time, which meant that their nakedness made them feel exposed rather than perfectly safe. In the relationship between people and God, distance had replaced intimacy. And in verses 14 and 15 God declares that humankind and the offspring of the devil will be locked in spiritual conflict—a battle between evil and good—with effects that will be seen throughout the verses that follow.

Second, the curse affects relationships between people. When God cursed the woman he did so almost entirely in relational contexts: "I will surely multiply your pain in childbearing; in pain you shall bring forth children. Your desire shall be contrary to your husband, but he shall rule over you" (3:16). While this focuses on the pain of childbirth and marital brokenness, it also entails something broader. Where once every human relationship was shaped like their relationship with God—in which they were naked, unashamed, guilt-free, honest, and safe—now they are marked by pain, sorrow, and conflict. Instead of caring for and serving one another, people seek to rule over and subjugate one another. Every human relationship is marked by this curse to some degree—friendships, marriages, parenting, co-working, neighboring. (Have you ever been on a neighborhood Facebook page? Whew.)

Third, we see the curse on people's relationship to creation. In Genesis 1 and 2 God commissioned Adam and Eve to care for, protect, and invest in creation: "Be fruitful and multiply and fill the earth and subdue it, and have dominion over the fish of the sea and over the birds of the heavens and over every living thing that moves on the earth" (1:28). Now Eve is told she will have pain in childbearing, so the task of being fruitful and multiplying becomes a hardship. Adam is told that the very ground will work against him by producing thorns and thistles (signifying any obstacle to productive, righteous, fruitful work). Instead of stewarding a creation that is entirely *good,* he must now wrestle with a creation that is cursed.

Finally, we see that people's relationship with the self is cursed. The text doesn't mention this explicitly, but as Scripture unfolds, it's clear that people have moved from a healthy and right understanding of the self to one that is skewed and broken. Before the fall, Adam and Eve were God's perfect image-bearers and looked to the one whose image they bore. They were able to view themselves as God viewed them—as whole, unique, loved, *good.* When their relationship with God went awry, it was inevitable that their view of self would too. They felt the need to hide themselves, first by covering their bodies and then by avoiding the presence of God (3:7, 10). Every human since has inherited this twisted view of self, sometimes believing too much of ourselves and sometimes too little.

Why does all this matter? Because you and I and everyone else are the offspring of Adam and Eve, so we carry in us their sinfulness. It is easy to look at the curse and think it is unfair because we didn't rebel in the garden, but we rebel every day. Romans 5:12 says, "Therefore, just as sin came into the world through one man, and death through sin, and so death spread to all men because all sinned…" We willfully reject the promises and commands of God by seeking to rule our own lives. We are very clearly Adam's offspring, so God's curse is rightfully on us too.

You likely knew all that already. The question is: do you live as though it's true?

CURSED HOPES

Last chapter we looked at the hooks on which we hang our hopes and expectations: the people, places, things, events, and circumstances we look to to deliver us happiness.

Here's the rub: every earthly object of hope is cursed. The hooks are broken—even the good ones. This means that there is no "perfect job," because every job is marred by the curse. There is no "perfect marriage," because every marriage is marred by the curse. If we're prone to expect life to be a bed of roses, Genesis 3 warns us to expect plenty of thorns.

But it's not just the *objects* of our hopes that are broken— our hopes and expectations *themselves* are too, because they are the products of hearts that have been bent out of shape by sin. Adam and Eve thought they knew better than God. They put their hopes in the lies of the devil and in their own decision-making ability. And we have been doing the same thing ever since. Our hopes are born from hearts passed down to us by Adam and Eve, and twisted by the lies we have believed. We trust ourselves, not God. Our feelings are our compass, and our intellects function as our steering wheel. But if those are marked by the curse, how much trust can we really put in our own hopes and expectations?

One way in which this plays out is in our approach to commitment. When it comes to work and church and relationships—those "hooks" we looked at last chapter—so often we allow our feelings to dictate our participation and commitment, and to cloud our long-term vision of what God wants for us. Since our hearts are sinful, we focus readily on immediate pleasures and desires, and fail to see things as God sees them. We miss his vision for community, stewardship, perseverance, or service. So when we follow our feelings, we will be perpetually abandoning things that God wants us to commit to because we hope for and expect the wrong things in the wrong timing from the wrong objects.

HOW CAN WE HOPE?

So if every thought and every effort springs from a cursed mind and heart, what hope have we of ever being free? None at all.

Except, that is, for this:

I will put enmity between you and the woman,
*   and between your offspring and her offspring;*
he shall bruise your head,
*   and you shall bruise his heel. (Genesis 3:15)*

Before God gave bad news, he gave the best news: the woman's offspring would be wounded by the serpent, but would strike a mortal blow in return. This is a promise of Christ's victory at the cross. Isaiah 53:5 echoes this language when it says, "But he was pierced for our transgressions; he was crushed for our iniquities." Jesus was the one whose heel was bruised, the one who was wounded, and the one whose death ensured Satan's death too.

What difference does this make for us? What does this change for us if we are still under the curse? Romans 6:5-8 says it so clearly:

For if we have been united with him in a death like his, we
shall certainly be united with him in a resurrection like his.
We know that our old self was crucified with him in order
that the body of sin might be brought to nothing, so that we
would no longer be enslaved to sin. For one who has died has
been set free from sin. Now if we have died with Christ, we
believe that we will also live with him.

We are set *free* from the power of sin. Yes, we are still fallen and still prone to rebel against God, but in Christ that is not our deepest, truest nature. In Christ we are made new and given a new heart—one that seeks after God. Sin no longer governs us; rather we have the Holy Spirit in us to overpower sin. In Christ we reflect the reality that God created in Eden: closeness to him, unity with one another, and redeemed work for the good of creation as we grow into the image of Christ.

And in Christ, in the power of the Holy Spirit, we are to "take every thought captive to obey Christ" (2 Corinthians 10:5).

This is the tall task set before every Christian, and at least part of it involves setting our hopes and expectations right. An uncaptured hope or expectation conspires to ruin our happiness.

To take thoughts captive is not just to fight against them or wrestle them into submission. The more we grapple with thoughts, the more they gain control of us. If I told you, "Don't think about crocodiles," what are you going to do? Think about crocodiles, of course. The only way to not think about something is to think about something else—something more captivating. Taking thoughts captive means to replace false ones with truer, better ones: to replace false hopes with hope in Christ.

As we do this, our expectations will get closer and closer to "just right." We will begin to hope for the right things from the right people. We will still place hopes in people and circumstances, but we will place biblically realistic hopes in them instead of twisted and outsized hopes that will break them and disappoint us.

Until Jesus returns, the earth will be marked, in its entirety, by the curse. We are the children of Adam and Eve in sin, but we also carry the marks of Eden. We are still wired to do work that matters, to care for creation by creating and protecting, to have meaningful relationships shaped by genuine love, and ultimately to pursue happiness in closeness with God. The curse took away our ability to have and do these things easily or perfectly or even at all. The good news of the gospel is that Jesus made a way for us to regain them. He has begun that work in his people today, and one day he will usher in a new creation that will be even better than Eden; on the day when, in the words of one old carol, "He comes to make his blessings flow far as the curse is found."

Until then, our hopes and expectations are shaped by the cursed present and the perfect future. In the present we must be gospel-oriented realists, and as we look toward the future we get to be gospel-fueled optimists. The curse ruins, but the curse is not permanent. So we temper our hopes for today and revel in our hopes for tomorrow.

CHAPTER 5

THAT'S ~~MY~~ GOD'S TRUTH

If we were looking for a single sentence to define our present day, a strong contender would be "That's my truth." It gets bandied about on social media, especially in debates over controversial subjects. You'll hear celebrities say it when discussing anything from personal faith to politics to the environment. People backstop their opinions or decisions with it. "That's my truth" says, *Truth is defined by me, and you cannot say otherwise.*

We live in a time when the idea of truth has become fluid. There is your truth, my truth, their truth, but we are generally uncomfortable with there being the truth. We want to define what is best for ourselves. And by defining "our truth," we think we define reality. We treat truth as something under our control: something malleable and multipurpose that can be put to work on our behalf. We bend language and modify meaning to suit our preferences and then state that something is "true" and therefore it must be real.

To quote one of my favorite television commercials, "That's not how it works. That's not how any of this works." (If you don't know the ad, google it.)

Reality just is. We don't get to define it. To attempt to do so is to step right into the shoes of our father Adam and our mother Eve. They decided that the reality God had created wasn't to their liking, and they sought to create a new "truth." And, well, we've seen where that got us. As creatures in our Father's world we have neither the right nor the ability to define reality. Reality exists as is, no matter what we say, and truth doesn't change even if we say it's "ours."

RECOGNIZING REALITY

What does this existential excursus have to do with happiness, you ask? Quite a bit, actually.

We've seen that the key to happiness is having the right expectations—of people, things, and the whole array of what life offers. But if we are under the delusion that truth is ours to define and reality will fall into line, our expectations for life will have no bearing on what is *actually* real and true. Rather than trying to shape reality with our expectations, we need to shape our expectations around reality as God has revealed it. That way we'll be saved from the misplaced expectations that lead to disappointment and profound unhappiness.

So it really matters that we have a firm grasp on reality and a clear definition of truth. And for that, we need the Bible.

STUFF THAT IS REAL

The Bible is God's flawless revelation of himself and his explanation of the how, what, and why of reality. It explains the author's intent behind the story of the universe and gives us a manual of sorts from the Creator as to how the creation is supposed to work.

But how can we be sure that the Bible really is the yardstick against which to measure our expectations? Because as we read Scripture, we see that it both *defines* reality and *reflects* reality. I was talking with a friend of mine recently whose wife had left him the year before. He, like me, had experienced the kind of pain and darkness that can obscure the goodness of God and make a person question the truth of the Bible. But instead, this friend had been white-knuckle-clinging to the words and promises of God through the entire heartbreaking mess. We talked for a while about our shared pain, the experience of walking through dark valleys, and God's constant goodness in leading us and carrying us. Then he said something so simple and profound that it actually made me laugh out loud: "Isn't it great how the Bible says stuff that is *real*?"

What he meant was that God's promises are true because they shape reality, and they shape reality because they are true. These words on a page make a difference to our experience in real life. They are the stuff and substance of every day hope. When we trust them and believe them, we actually see them play out on a Tuesday afternoon when we are crushed by guilt and shame, but then we remember that "there is therefore now no condemnation for those who are in Christ Jesus" (Romans 8:1). We see their reality on a Sunday morning when we can barely drag ourselves to church because of loneliness and depression, but then we walk into the warm smile and embrace of a friend and remember that Jesus said that in him we would gain innumerable brothers and mothers and sisters (Mark 10:30). We know their truth in the middle of a sleepless, anxious night when the reality of Christ's presence never leaving or forsaking us gives us enough peace to roll over and rest (Hebrews 13:5).

The Bible is a book of cosmic wonders, theological profundities, and eternal mysteries—but it's also a book for real life. Or rather, that is *how* it is a book for real life. Those depths make a difference today.

DEFINING EXPECTATIONS BY TRUTH

To have healthy expectations means disposing of "my truth" and living according to *the truth,* which God has revealed in his word. "The words of the LORD are pure words, like silver refined in a furnace on the ground, purified seven times" (Psalm 12:6).

A helpful way to think about truth is to define it as "reality as God intends it to be." There are at least three senses to this. Scripture reflects the reality that God created before the fall (his intent for creation), the reality after the fall (his intentional curse on the world), and the reality that is to come in the new creation (his glorious final intent for eternity).

To understand truth this way gives us a clear understanding of the reality that is now. *Reality as God intends* is broken under his curse and is hopeful because of his Son. It also gives us an understanding of God's desire for the world. *Reality as God intends* takes the shape of his Son's kingdom, under his authority and shaped by his will—so we live rightly when we reflect our King in humility, self-sacrifice, and compassion for lost people. And truth points us to what will be in the future. *Reality as God intends* will be redeemed and purified. Jesus will return and usher in a new earth unmarked by any curse, and all who believe will be part of this world.

Here's the key idea for this chapter: we should shape our actions and expectations according to reality as God intends it to be, in all three senses.

So we should relate to *people*—and expect of them—according to reality as God intends it to be. This means realizing that every person is an image-bearer of our Creator and worthy of respect and love, while also recognizing their inherent sinfulness and ability to do evil. We can neither withdraw into sheltered skepticism about humanity nor fall into the trap of believing that people are inherently good. This is why we lean so heavily on grace, forgiveness, and honesty to make healthy relationships happen.

We should create and enjoy *art* and *work*—and expect of them—according to reality as God intends it to be. This means artists should be willing to reflect the hardship, pain, and evil in the world, but in a manner that doesn't glorify it. And they should reflect the beauty and wonders of God's good world too. Workers should strive to accomplish all we can, while remembering that no accomplishment will ever fulfill us. The work of our hands—be it a shingled roof, a sonnet, or a tray of cookies—innately reflects God's creativity in us. And as we as God's people put our hands to work with the aim of honoring Christ, that will further shape what we do and how we do it.

We should view and understand *ourselves*—and expect of ourselves—according to reality as God intends it to be: as people who are "in Christ." So we throw ourselves on the mercy of Christ, define our value as someone in Christ, pursue Christ-likeness, and depend on Christ moment by moment. Any other definition of ourselves is hopeless, putting us outside God's intent for us.

To be happy we must live in reality—we must be true realists. It is not simple or always clear how to do it, and there are inherent tensions. But defining our expectations any other way—especially by "my truth"—will run contrary to the reality God created and God intends.

HOW THE BIBLE GOVERNS ALL REALITY

Sometimes, though, reality as God has revealed it in the Bible won't be reality as we'd like it. Perhaps his rules look restrictive or his commands seem demanding. The call to die to self feels like it sounds... death. It's easy to start thinking, "If only God would let me do X, I would be happier." Or even, "I would be happier if I did X, so God must let me."

In my final year of high school I had a literature teacher who told the class that of equal importance to an author's intent was the reader's interpretation. So, he argued, it matters just as much what we read into a text as it does what the author meant.

As an author I take great umbrage at this. As a Christian I take even more. Yet quite often this is how we approach the Bible—we bring our preferences and opinions and look in Scripture for evidence to support them. Then we take what we like and leave behind what we don't.

But again, "That's not how it works. That's not how any of this works." 2 Timothy 3:16 tells us that "*all* Scripture is breathed out by God and profitable for teaching, for reproof, for correction, and for training in righteousness" (my emphasis). The Bible is unerring and non-accidental. It is intentional in every syllable.

More than this, though, when we find parts we don't like or that conflict with our version of happiness, we must remember that the words of Scripture *came to life* in the person of Jesus. He is the Word, who became flesh (John 1:14). Jesus is the embodied word of God: the revelation of God's good news of salvation. It means that every word of the Bible is about Jesus; if we want to understand it, we can only do that through him. And it means that if we want to know Jesus, we encounter him first and foremost through the Bible.

Further, it means we don't have authority over any part of scripture. The Bible defines truth and shapes reality. When we attempt to wrest control, we are attempting to gain authority over Jesus, our King, and seeking to alter reality as God intends it to be.

But when we hear and accept Jesus' words, we find joy. In John 14:6 he says, "I am the way, and the truth, and the life." Jesus' truth is the way to life because he is life—life in abundance (John 10:10). His words bring joy to all who will accept them. And he gives us the Spirit, our "Helper" and teacher, so that we can understand the words of God (John 14:25-27; 16:7-15). When we read the Bible, we find it is not dry and abstract; it is powerful and personal. The Spirit empowers us and enables us to obey Scripture.

He lives *in* followers of Jesus; he is the presence of God in us (1 Corinthians 3:16). He knows the mind of God and transforms the hearts of people to be like Jesus. And he "helps us in our weakness" to pray, as we walk in relationship with God (Romans 8:26). Every follower of Jesus has the Spirit in him or her, and there is no following Jesus without the Spirit. Without the Spirit we are not able. With the Spirit we are unable not to.

Scripture is the written truth of God—the same truth that is embodied in Jesus and written on our hearts by the Spirit. It is reality. It is *the* truth. So we can turn from "our truth" to rest in and follow the words of Proverbs 3:5-8:

> *Trust in the LORD with all your heart,*
> *and do not lean on your own understanding.*
> *In all your ways acknowledge him,*
> *and he will make straight your paths.*
> *Be not wise in your own eyes;*
> *fear the LORD, and turn away from evil.*
> *It will be healing to your flesh*
> *and refreshment to your bones.*

What a corrective for our expectations. What a lens through which to view life. What a place of calm in the midst of the scramble to discover and take hold of the next temporal happiness. God's word is true and real. It is real because it is true, and it is true because it is his. And that means we can trust it with all our heart, all our hopes, and all our expectations, and take deep joy in "how the Bible says stuff that is real."

CHAPTER 6

EVANGELIGUILT

Growing up in conservative American Christianity I encountered a cultural phenomenon that never felt quite right to me. I call it "evangeliguilt"—a perpetual low-grade guilt about enjoying things. It seems to have its roots in a modern-day perception of the Puritans—our 17th-century spiritual forebears—as dour, sour, no-fun, dry-bread-gnawing, lukewarm-water-sipping killjoys. Since the Puritans are so seminally important in our church history, this perception has flavored our ability to enjoy good things today.

Evangeliguilt is not outright skepticism about fun or happiness or pleasure. Rather, it exhibits itself much more in the tendency to make excuses for fun or to temper descriptions of enjoyable experiences so that they don't sound too lavish or expensive. It's evangeliguilt that makes people say things like "I enjoy a glass of wine with dinner," when what they really mean is that they have an impressive wine cellar and appreciate a good Malbec with steak or a Sauvignon Blanc with whitefish. Other times it is revealed in response to a compliment. You might say "Oh, that is a nice jacket," and the response will be quick-draw fast: "Thanks, I found it on sale!" so as not to let you think they bought a name-brand item at full price. By minimizing the impression of our indulgence in this way, we also avoid falling victim to other people's evangeliguilt—that silent judgement on another's "lack of stewardship" and the fact that they really could have used that money to bless others.

Evangeliguilt applies to our work ethic too. We must earn leisure through hard work (what is often called a "Puritan work ethic"), almost as if there is a ratio we must follow: eight hours of hard work earns one hour of relaxation, or something like that. We also have to earn our caloric intake by being consistent in working out. Even on a day like Thanksgiving, we feel we have to go for a morning run to earn a right to feast. And vacations? In our guilt-ridden minds those are stressful interruptions in exhausting work schedules that just create more work when we get back. And we had better not give the impression that we spent too much money on them either.

Almost none of this is expressed directly. It is much more of a gut feeling of guilt and a quiet sense of skepticism toward other, more ostentatious people (even as we feel jealous of their freedom to just *enjoy*).

In one sense, evangeliguilt is actually a twisted offshoot of good theology: belief in man's sinfulness and our propensity to idolize things and expect too much of them. But somehow this proper theological emphasis has been misapplied so as to diminish our enjoyment of cheeseburgers and movies and dancing and laughter and myriad other delights of life. Somehow our awareness of sin and fallenness has made us suspicious of fully enjoying anything.

This is a problem, and not just because it's a drag. It's a problem because it's not how the Bible depicts the way life should be.

GOOD GIFTS, GOOD WORLD, GOD'S GLORY

In contrast to our evangeliguilt, James 1:17 says, "Every good gift and every perfect gift is from above, coming down from the Father of lights, with whom there is no variation or shadow due to change." I love this verse because of the constancy and generosity it depicts in God. He is the giver of *all good things*, and he will not change. He is not a capricious giver prone to whims or mood swings. He is a provider rich with goodness for his followers.

At the same time, it's easy to grab verses like this and slap them on anything we like in order to say "See? It's from God!" as a sort of spiritual trump card to back up our preferences and desires. But we don't get to define what counts as a "good gift" or how we use it. Instead we need to look across the whole of Scripture to get a picture of how God wants us to engage with and *enjoy* his good gifts.

As Julie Andrews once sang in *The Sound of Music*: "Let's start at the very beginning, a very good place to start." Genesis 1 lays the foundation for understanding what these good and perfect gifts are. Time and again as God spoke creation into being, he declared it "good." This isn't a term of comparison, as in "good-better-best." This is "good" as in exactly what God intended: perfect. The world God created was not ok or decent or fine; it was exactly right. It was *good*.

We've already looked at all that went wrong with the world (Genesis 3). But what we often forget is that sin and the curse did not evaporate the good and replace it. They did not recreate the world as a heinously evil hellscape. Sin corrupted the good, but the world still has God's fingerprints all over it and tendrils of Eden woven through it. Nothing is completely as it should be, but neither is the world utterly corrupt. The good that once defined all of creation still shines throughout it.

In the film *The Lord of the Rings: The Two Towers*, Sam Gamgee and Frodo Baggins have a memorable conversation as they struggle toward Mount Doom. Frodo is ready to give up because the burden is too heavy and the journey too perilous. Sam's response is profound: "There's some good in this world, Mr. Frodo, and it's worth fighting for."

In some situations it really does feel that we must search for the good and persuade ourselves it will be worth fighting for. But there is more than just "some good" in this world; there is an abundance if we would open our eyes, discard our evangeliguilt, and recognize that this is still God's creation. It is still the creation of the Father of lights, from whom every good and perfect gift comes.

And Christians are invited to get in on the fun: "So, whether you eat or drink, or whatever you do, do all to the glory of God"(1 Corinthians 10:31). Notice how Paul is focusing on the stuff of everyday life, not just grand endeavors. When I read this, my first instinct is to cringe because it feels like I need to be *serious* about every little action. It sounds burdensome to be obliged to please God with my sandwiches and my black coffee. But that mindset is another misapplication of good theology. To glorify God in my eating and drinking (or whatever I do) doesn't necessarily mean I need to be serious. It means I need to be purposeful. It means that I need to pay attention to the goodness in this world because "the earth is the Lord's, and everything in it" (v 26, NIV). It means eating "with thankfulness" (v 30) and embracing joy, which glorifies God.

GOD MADE THINGS GOOD FOR US

Scripture is rife with evidence of God's lavish goodness to us. (Remember Jesus turning water into wine so the party could keep on rocking? Not to mention more than a few references to fatted calf roasts in the Gospels.) Let's look at a few other passages to see what "good and perfect gifts" we are invited to revel in.

First, Scripture rejoices in tangible and edible gifts from God. Psalm 104 is a 35-verse song of praise. It looks first at God's personal glory as King of the universe and then turns its attention to the beauty and majesty of creation, including the consumable, earthly gifts that God gives us.

You cause the grass to grow for the livestock
  and plants for man to cultivate,
that he may bring forth food from the earth
  and wine to gladden the heart of man,
oil to make his face shine
  and bread to strengthen man's heart. (Psalm 104:14-15)

This is not a grocery list of items for which the writer is grateful but a sweeping meditation that revels in God's provision. It is *good* to enjoy food. It is *good* to be glad in drink. It is *good* to care for ourselves by giving attention to health and hygiene, and to present ourselves well (what the writer means by "oil to make his face shine"). *Good* like Eden, like God intended.

Scripture shows us the goodness of joy in relationships too. Proverbs 5:18 says to "rejoice in the wife of your youth." Song of Solomon is an entire book of love poetry between a man and a woman who end up as husband and wife. In each of his letters, Paul greets friends and gives thanks for them in a way that shows he views them with deep affection. The story of David and Jonathan in 1 Samuel and the portrayal of Jesus' warmth toward his disciples in the Gospels demonstrate friendships that are close and meaningful and genuine. Love and close human relationships are means of God's *goodness* and reflect what God intended in Eden.

We see the pleasure of work throughout the Bible too. Ecclesiastes 9:10 says, "Whatever your hand finds to do, do it with your might." Why—because God is a taskmaster? No—because there is fulfillment and pleasure in work done well and time well-spent. When God commanded Moses to have a tabernacle built for him in Exodus, he did not just give him specifications, a budget, and a time frame. He gave instructions for the lavish and rich materials to be used, the intricate patterns to be followed, the purpose of each item, and how they all fit together. There were even parts of the tabernacle that could not be seen by human eyes but were crafted with skill and beauty because God took pleasure in them! God gave special skills to the craftsmen and artists who built his house. God cares about work, craft, and creativity because it is *good* and in it we should find happiness.

We also see Bible writers gushing with praise (happiness) about the wonders of nature: "The heavens declare the glory of God, and the sky above proclaims his handiwork" (Psalm 19:1). We see music portrayed as a means of joyous expression: "Praise him with trumpet sound; praise him with lute and harp! Praise him with tambourine and dance; praise him with strings and pipe! Praise him with sounding cymbals; praise him with loud clashing cymbals!" (Psalm 150:3-5). And the Bible ends in Revelation with a great wedding feast for Christ and his church. From its beginning to end—*good* creation to new creation—the Bible tells of enjoyment and goodness and richness. Why? Because God is the giver of all good gifts, and in him "there is no variation or shadow due to change."

EAT, DRINK, AND BE MERRY BECAUSE GOD SAID SO

All this does come with a warning, though. Evangeliguilt is the bane of some of us, but idolatry is the bane of all of us. We have a tendency to take temporal things and elevate them to objects of worship and hope. Usually we do this with good things, like the weak hooks we discussed in chapter 3. We can turn food, drink, work, relationships, and health, and nearly any other good gift from God into an idol. Many of us who feel that sense of suspicion at enjoyment do so precisely because we know our propensity for idolatry. We know we can turn good things into objects of worship, so we are skeptical of enjoying the good things. But this is the wrong response. It's true that God is not honored by us idolizing his gifts—but nor is he honored by our ignoring them.

Ecclesiastes attacks both false notions with all the vigor of an artillery barrage. It bids us appreciate good gifts *precisely because* they come from the perfect giver; one is never without the other.

> *There is nothing better for a person than that he should eat and drink and find enjoyment in his toil. This also, I saw, is from the hand of God, for apart from him who can eat or who can have enjoyment? (Ecclesiastes 2:24-25)*

Eat, drink, enjoy your work, enjoy your loved ones, enjoy the brightness of the sun—these are commands from God. There is no room for idolatry if we constantly come back to the giver—acknowledging that *God* gives life, gives food, gives enjoyment—and to eternity. These good gifts are for our pleasure *now*, but we're fools if we depend on them to fulfill our eternal hopes.

Yet neither are we to be suspicious of the gifts God gives. There is no room for guilt or evasion. There is no place for asceticism: the idea that eschewing pleasure will lead to greater holiness. Not having fun is no grounds for spiritual superiority.

In his book *Living Life Backward*, David Gibson explains it like this:

> *"Pleasure is a divine decree that we ignore at our peril. For it is precisely in enjoying the world God has made that we show we have grasped the goodness of the God we say we love. Failure to enjoy is an offense, not merely an oversight ... Not to live gladly, joyfully, and not drink deeply from the wells of abundant goodness that God has lavished on us, is sin, and it is sin because it is a denial of who he is."*

We saw already that a failure to realistically recognize hardship and disappointment is to deny the curse of Genesis 3. However, a failure to revel in God's *good* gifts is to repeat the very sin that brought about the curse: claiming that we know better than God what is good for us.

FREEDOM IN CHRIST, FREEDOM LIKE CHRIST

It seems almost impossible to walk the line between avoiding earthly pleasures and worshiping earthly pleasures. I am constantly pulled between the two, swinging like a pendulum—but there are two realities I've learned to hold on to that help me.

The first is the reality of freedom in Jesus. 2 Corinthians 5:17 says, "Therefore, if anyone is in Christ, he is a new creation. The old has passed away; behold, the new has come." A believer in Jesus is *in* Christ. That phrase, "in Christ," is vast and transformative, but one of the things it means is that our identity has changed. Christ defines us, so we no longer need to try to fill ourselves up or make ourselves into something. Instead we have freedom like we never had before: freedom from slavery to sin (including idolatry), freedom from guilt, freedom from shame, and freedom to live like Jesus without being defined or beaten down by the judgments and criticisms of the world.

Jesus himself received plenty of judgment, especially from conservative religious folks. In Matthew 11:19 he said of himself, "The Son of Man came eating and drinking, and they say, 'Look at him! A glutton and a drunkard, a friend of tax collectors and sinners!' Yet wisdom is justified by her deeds." He faced criticism from the conservative religious crowd of his day for his enjoyment of people and his use of God's good gifts. But we know he did not idolize or over-indulge or base his hope for happiness in them. He simply enjoyed earthly things and used them as a means to connect with those he had come to save.

God's good gifts are at our disposal to enjoy as Jesus enjoyed them—often and with pleasure, even to the point of making the guilt-mongers uncomfortable. And we are free to use these gifts as Jesus used them—to connect with others and show the goodness of God to those who don't yet know him. A laughing Christian who relishes good things is a compelling, magnetic Christian—the kind who draws people to truth.

The second reality that keeps me from false guilt and keeps me from idolatry is gratitude. I mentioned earlier that glorifying God in eating, drinking, or whatever we do is not so much about being serious as about being intentional. What that really means is that we must be intentionally grateful. Gratitude never diminishes pleasure, and it always glorifies God. If we find ourselves unable to be grateful for a good thing, it probably means that something is out of alignment in our hearts (or we know that the thing isn't really good for us). If we are thankful to God for something, then we cannot feel guilty about enjoying it. And if we are truly thankful to God for something, we will not use it in a manner that twists his intent for it.

In *Chariots of Fire*, the 1981 film about Scottish Olympic runner Eric Liddell, Eric faces the difficult decision between following God's call to be a missionary in China or running in the 1924 Olympics. His sister makes it clear that she believes he should abandon running and go to China straight away, but Liddell eventually decides to compete in the Olympics, telling her, "I believe God made me for a purpose, for China, but he also made me fast. And when I run I feel his pleasure!"

There is something rich and right about this whole exchange. Liddell knows his purpose, as a Christian, is to show people Jesus (and after the Olympics he did go to China as a missionary for the rest of his life). He also recognizes that God gave him a good gift, speed, and that it can be used both for pleasure and God's glory. He feels pleasure when running fast and racing, and he simultaneously feels God's pleasure at seeing one of his children relishing a good gift.

In real life, as in the film, Liddell did not cave in to the potential for guilt and give up his gift. Neither did he use it for personal glory or some other idolatrous end. Instead, he saw that it was from God, gave thanks for it, and took joy in it, and by doing so glorified God in it. This is how God's good gifts are to be enjoyed by his children.

CHAPTER 7

LIVING IN TIMES OF TROUBLE

It is easy to think of the good and bad in the world, the gifts and the curse, as a sort of scale. For every good there will be something bad to balance it out, and for every season of joy there will be a season of pain or sorrow. The ancient Chinese philosophy of yin and yang speaks to this idea of the universe balancing itself—dark and light, male and female, good and evil, and so on. It proposes that the world is made up of two competing but equal forces or energies that balance each other in the end.

In Hinduism and Buddhism, the concept of karma is that good actions lead to good effects for you, and bad actions lead to pain. This creates a sort of moral order, since everything a person experiences they deserve for some reason or another. The cause and effect of actions can be passed down from generation to generation. In the secular West, we tend to believe something pretty similar: "You get what you deserve." We don't necessarily think in terms of karmic outcomes, but we do believe in good actions leading to good and bad actions leading to pain. It just seems right and fair.

Every major religion or belief system rests on an adjacent belief system that explains good and evil, and gives people some sense of moral direction. Christianity, however, differs significantly. Our beliefs about good and evil, morality and immorality are not tied to undefined competing cosmic forces, fickle and difficult-to-please gods, or karmic outcomes. We believe in a perfectly good, sovereign God, who governs all. We believe in his justice, mercy, and infinite wisdom in ruling all things, even evil ones.

This means that we are free to respond to the hardships (and joys) of life differently than others. Last chapter we saw how God gives good gifts and how we get to enjoy them. This chapter we'll look at the harder parts of life and how we get to (and must) respond as Christians.

TWO KINDS OF PROMISES

If I asked you to list some promises of God, what would be your go-to passages of Scripture?

I'm guessing that most of us would go straight to Scripture's words of hope and restoration—gems like these:

> *I will never leave you nor forsake you. (Hebrews 13:5)*

> *Be strong and courageous. Do not be frightened, and do not be dismayed, for the LORD your God is with you wherever you go. (Joshua 1:9)*

> *I will strengthen you, I will help you, I will uphold you with my righteous right hand. (Isaiah 41:10)*

> *And we know that for those who love God all things work together for good, for those who are called according to his purpose. (Romans 8:28)*

> *The LORD is my Shepherd; I shall not want. (Psalm 23:1)*

The list could go on and on because the Bible overflows with promises. But I'm guessing you'd be slower to point to this promise, straight from the mouth of Jesus:

I have told you these things, so that in me you may have peace. In this world you will have trouble. But take heart! I have overcome the world. (John 16:33, NIV)

It starts out like the sort of promise we're accustomed to and it ends like one too, but what's that in the middle? It's a promise of tribulation—but a promise nonetheless.

Jesus spoke these words to his disciples on the night he was arrested and condemned to death. He was warning them that to follow him would bring persecution from the Jewish religious leaders—they were about to kill him, and before long they would be out to kill his friends. Jesus knew that his arrest and crucifixion would terrify the disciples and scatter them, so he left them with hope they could cling to. But it's hope set in the reality of what life in "this world" looks like.

Persecution is all part of the plan, Jesus says, *One day I will return and rule and do away with all evil. But in the meantime, you will have trouble in this fallen, sinful world that rejects the gospel.*

COMING TO GRIPS

We've looked long at how happiness depends on having right expectations in life (chapters 2 and 3). Jesus' words in John 16 define one of the things we must expect from life, especially life following Jesus: suffering. To expect otherwise is to be naive or to willfully disregard God's word.

Those of us who grew up in comfortable middle-class homes in the West find this particularly hard to comprehend. My parents were present, loving, and provided for my every need (though not my every wish). I was able to participate in sports and activities; we traveled some as a family; our home was a veritable library; there were gifts at each birthday and Christmas; and our pantry and refrigerator were well-stocked. Aside from a couple of dust-ups with neighborhood bullies, the only times I ever felt threatened were when my older brothers decided I was a perfect lab rat or punching bag. In short, I lived a life of ease and safety and comfort.

My parents also faithfully taught me the Bible—the *whole* Bible. They told me that I would likely suffer for following Jesus, and they taught me about counting the cost of being his disciple (Luke 14:25-33). But I was *comfortable*. I lived in a place where we had freedom of religion and religious expression. There was no visible cost to being a disciple. I believed what they told me, but in the same way that I believe a mathematician when she says the square root of 11,000,000 is 3316.625. I was confident that it was true, but I had no idea why it really mattered or how to figure it out myself. I was naive and shrugged off God's words.

But life has a way of bringing the truth of Scripture into stark reality. The pervasive presence of the curse from Genesis 3 forces us to confront life's trouble. For many people throughout the world, this trouble takes the form of a daily threat to their well-being specifically for following Jesus, just as Jesus warned his disciples would be the case in John 16. For most of us in the West, our trouble isn't overt persecution for our faith but rather the more "general" pain of living in a world of suffering, betrayal, loss, and doubt. As we saw in chapter 4, all is broken and that means that we will have trouble in every area of life in one form or another.

For me, trouble has come as a consequence of my own sins, which led to a job loss and near financial destitution. It's come in the form of a crisis of faith, when the shallow belief of my youth confronted deep and mysterious questions about God. It has come through difficult, and occasionally miserable, professional circumstances. It has come in a deteriorating marriage that came to a painful end. It continues to come daily as I am confronted with all the ways in which I am a sinner and a failure. It comes in seeing my inadequacy as a father to my two daughters. It comes in feeling unqualified and an ill fit as minister at my church.

I'm sure you have faced trouble too. Some of it will have been of your own making, but some of it will have been outside your control. Perhaps you have been treated unjustly; or you have battled mental or physical health issues, lost loved ones, seen financial markets send your livelihood up in smoke, or suffered myriad other life-ravaging experiences. We've all experienced trouble, and we'll continue to experience trouble. It shouldn't surprise us.

1 Peter 4:12 offers a strong dose of biblical realism to that effect:

> *Beloved, do not be surprised at the fiery trial when it comes upon you to test you, as though something strange were happening to you.*

Peter's words echo those of his Lord from years earlier. We should expect trouble. But here's the thing: we don't. We're usually shocked by suffering because we fail to believe Scripture's blunt words or believe they only apply to others. But the Bible says trouble is a certainty, and our experience proves it.

This unpleasant reality raises a pointed question: how can we be happy in the midst of all this difficulty?

The answer is found back where we started: in the promises of God.

FUTURE HOPE IS PAST REALITY

In our pursuit of happiness in this troubled life, it's easy to fall into one of two errors as we think about God's promises. The first is to think we can "claim" them in some manner that puts us in control of their outcome. So when something has gone awry, we find a promise that seems to offer an improvement to life and we "name it and claim it" for the desired outcome. When we do this, we try to wield God's promises as tools to build a better life. We act as if we know best when and how a promise should play out. We ignore the entire premise that God is sovereign and has a plan of which all his promises are part, and we go back to the sin of Adam and Eve and begin playing God.

The other error is to treat promises, especially the promises of hope and blessing, as applying only to the distant future. This mindset focuses on "some day" rather than recognizing the goodness and presence of God and the fulfillment of his promises now. It looks toward heaven and the second coming of Jesus, but leapfrogs over the life that will occur between now and then. In the end it leaves us with the mindset of enduring this life just to get to the next, as if these troubled years are the dues we pay in order to earn glory. So we grin and bear it through the difficulty, without expecting God to deliver on his promises in any real way.

Think back to recent hardships in your life: which side do you tend to err on? Whichever it is, if you have swung too far one way or the other, you've missed out on the fullness of hope God has given us in his promises. When we seek to own a promise or we push it off into the distant future, we actually diminish the life, death, and resurrection of Jesus. Why? Because neither of these errors rest in what Jesus has accomplished. 2 Corinthians 1:20 says:

For all the promises of God find their Yes in him. That is why it is through him that we utter our Amen to God for his glory.

Jesus is the fulfillment and the means of fulfillment for all God's promises of good for us. Think back to how John 16:33 concludes: "But take heart; I have overcome the world." Even before he went to the cross, Jesus was saying, *It is finished.* His victory was sure. By living sinlessly, dying innocently, rising from the grave to conquer death, and ascending to sit at God's right as our intercessor, he gives us hope and happiness for *today*, not just some day. Remember, "the Bible says stuff that is real." The victory of Jesus matters for a Tuesday afternoon when the baby won't sleep, a Friday night of anxious insomnia, a Sunday service crushed by the tonnage of shame, or a holiday when the absence of a loved one feels like an amputation. When it feels like everything else is spiraling out of control, we trust that Christ is on his throne, weaving the threads of our lives into the pattern he intends.

As Christians we should always have an eye to the future, to the coming of Jesus. We should rest in the assurance that someday all this trouble we were promised and are experiencing will be wiped away. We should remember that "this light momentary affliction is preparing for us an eternal weight of glory beyond all comparison" (2 Corinthians 4:17). But our future hope does not entail a mere act of waiting and pining. Yes, we yearn and ache for our true home with Christ, and when life is at its worst, our ache is the deepest. But we also *live* now, and live fully, because our assurance for the future is in the past (John 10:10). We know that Jesus will come again because he already won the battle over sin and death on that first Good Friday and Easter Sunday. We live between Christ's first coming and his final coming, and this means we have the hope we need to truly live even as we wait.

TRULY LIVING IN TIMES OF TROUBLE

But what does it mean to truly live in a world full of trouble? This is one of those times when we especially need to see how Scripture speaks to the grit and grind of life.

At least part of it comes back to enjoying God's good gifts. Last chapter we saw how Scripture encourages enjoyment and pleasure, and those don't cease in the midst of pain and trouble. In fact, those are the times when the good gifts of God matter most because they remind us of his present love and ongoing goodness to us. Yet in times of trouble, our inclination will often be to either abuse or ignore these gifts from God.

Sometimes we will want to inoculate ourselves to the pain, so we binge bourbon or Ben and Jerry's. Sometimes we want a cocoon to hide in, so we curl up inside the safety of stories told by Netflix or Hulu. But if we are replacing the giver with the gifts and depending on the gifts to do what only the giver can, then something has gone wrong in our hearts—we've moved from appreciation to idolatry.

The other side of this that suffering diminishes our ability to enjoy God's good gifts. In times of trouble we lose our appetites. We withdraw from friends. We lose motivation at work. We stop laughing. Can a joke or a drink or a job solve our woes? No, but they are one means through which God gives happiness in the midst of trouble. They are like his "Get Well Soon" or "Just Thinking of You" card. So over time we seek to taste and laugh and love and work, even as we cry and hurt and struggle.

These good gifts are not separate from the good news of Jesus unless we separate them. It is not "theology" vs. "all that other stuff," unless we remove that other stuff from the realm of Jesus' victory. In a very real, everyday sense, the good gifts God gives on earth are deeper and richer and better because of Jesus. Because of Jesus, we don't have to depend on them, but rather we are free to enjoy them. Because of Jesus, we don't need to hoard them but are free to share them. Because of Jesus, we are free to enjoy them but not fear them. And because of Jesus, we can find happiness in them even when life is terrible, because we know the giver and we know life will not always be terrible.

The Bible reframes happiness for us by complexifying it. We tend to think of being happy or sad, but Scripture depicts a sort of happiness in the midst of sadness. In this life we will have trouble, but in this life we will have happiness. And this doesn't mean being on an emotional yo-yo (even though it will sometimes feel that way), but rather experiencing two things at once: one being the damage caused by sin and the other being the happiness given by God. This happiness, true happiness, is rooted in Jesus. Through his work on the cross we have the assurance of Christ's presence in the midst of our troubles and the promise that one day "he will wipe away every tear from their eyes, and death shall be no more, neither shall there be mourning, nor crying, nor pain anymore, for the former things have passed away" (Revelation 21:4).

Our incomplete, marred, temporary happiness looks ahead to that day. But being incomplete, marred, and temporary doesn't make it a farce. In Jesus our happiness is deep and real, even as we face the troubles of life.

CHAPTER 8

DON'T FEAR THE REAPER

As the old saying goes, there are two certainties in life: death and taxes. The unspoken subtext is that we'd all like to avoid them but can't. Sure, you can duck the Internal Revenue Service and cheat on your taxes. But when it comes to death, there are no offshore accounts, hidden assets, or fudged income statements. You can't cheat death. It comes for us all.

It seems that the general reaction to death, at least in Western culture, is that of a young child playing hide and seek. When my daughters were toddlers, they would "hide" by putting towels over their heads or wedging their torsos behind a bookshelf with their diapered backsides sticking out. They assumed that if they couldn't see me, I couldn't see them. And Westerners are basically toddlers when it comes to death—if we hide our faces and don't see it, then it won't find us.

This leads to an odd and irreconcilable tension, as people go to great lengths to hide themselves from a thing they deny is a reality. It's like putting bars on the windows of your home and installing a state-of-the-art alarm system to protect against burglars, while never acknowledging that they actually exist. Entire industries are built on the "promise" of fending off mortality. A new fitness cult, er, regimen, becomes popular every few months. Different diets insist that gluten, dairy, meat, legumes, sugar, grains, fruits, poultry, and fish will all kill you. (They somehow all agree that kale and water are safe and acceptable—depressing, really.) The cosmetic and beauty industry is gargantuan as people hide graying hair, crow's feet, laugh lines, love handles, varicose veins, and the effects of gravity on various parts of the body. We glorify youth by marginalizing aging and the aged—both diminishing the status of those who should receive the most respect and diminishing ourselves by discarding their decades of wisdom and experience—because we want to avoid the obvious evidence of death drawing near.

Hiding our faces from death doesn't change reality. It doesn't forestall the inevitable. We're under the impression that denying the existence of this sad reality will somehow increase our happiness (willful ignorance is bliss?), but it doesn't. Quite the opposite: it only diminishes and dilutes the meaning and fullness of life that God intends.

BACKDROP AND BORDER

In the 1991 film *What About Bob?* (one of the smartest and funniest movies of my lifetime), uber neurotic and unstable Bob Wiley befriends the family of his psychologist, the perfectly smug and superior Leo Marvin. When Bob crashes the Marvin family's New Hampshire lake vacation, a thunderstorm forces him to spend the night with them against the wishes of Dr. Marvin. In a scene that would make parents of today more than a little uncomfortable, forty-something Bob shares a room with the Marvin's middle-school-aged son Siggy (named after Sigmund Freud, of course). Siggy is a brooding boy who wears only black and has a fixation with death. This late-night conversation ensues:

Siggy: "Bob, are you afraid of death?"

Bob: "Yeah."

Siggy: "Me too, but there's no way out of it. You're going to die. I'm going to die. It's going to happen, and what difference does it make if it's tomorrow or eighty years … much sooner in your case. Do you know how fast time goes? I was six, like, yesterday."

Bob: "Me too."

Siggy: "I'm going to die. You are going to die. What else is there to be afraid of?"

I wouldn't go so far as to call Siggy Marvin's perspective healthy, but there is much to be said for the clarity with which he views life. He sees what so many people refuse to: the inevitability of death and the shortness of life. We could all learn from Siggy and come to terms with the fact that "You're going to die. I'm going to die." Death is, in fact, our defining earthly reality. And if we embrace the fact of our mortality in the right way, it can actually lead us toward happiness.

So what does that look like? For one thing, death is the backdrop against which every expectation, hope, and choice should be viewed. We do not choose and think and plan in a space of infinite opportunity and a million chances. Our expectations cannot expand out to undefined horizons and possibilities. Our relationships and resources have an endpoint. Everything we do is cast against our pending mortality, and that should shape what we pursue and how we pursue it. It adds urgency and focus to how we prioritize our money and our minutes. It clarifies what and who truly matters in our lives and offers a sharp reminder that every person is on the clock and we should treat them accordingly. Rightly understood, the reality of death bulldozes lethargy and listlessness to give us focus and direction, by motivating us to use the lifespan God has given us for the purposes he prioritizes.

Another way to think about it is that death is the set of borders that contains our lives. Sometimes borders feel like captivity, like a prison wall. Sometimes borders are for our own good, like lane lines on the road. And sometimes borders are just the rules of the game, as on a Monopoly or Scrabble board. Death defines the rules of the game of life. It is the statute of limitations on every earthly action and hope and expectation.

This means that to fully live, to fully embrace happiness, we must acknowledge and accept death. *Wait! Come again?! To be happy we must accept death?!* Yes, because to be truly happy we must have right expectations and recognize the world both as it is and as God intends it to be. Otherwise we spend our lives pretending and ignoring and deluding ourselves until our final day comes with such a shockwave that everything we have done and built and hoped for crumbles. To ignore death is to create an alternate reality built on false hopes, in which the only happiness is a figment.

HAPPINESS AND DEATH

"But death hurts," you might be thinking. "It's stolen away people I love. Death is an enemy we can't defeat." Those things are also true. Saying we can only find true happiness *in light of death* is not the same as saying we can only find happiness *in* death or that death *makes us* happy. We should absolutely hate death—it's an evil which came about because of sin. But we must also accept the reality of death as inevitable and in God's hands. Only when we accept it can we play by the rules of life, set true expectations, and find the happiness God has for us this side of heaven.

Once we come to terms with the reality of mortality, it does something to our perspective. Last chapter we looked at how we live between Christ's earthly ministry and his return, and how we should have an eye to the future and our anchor in the past. Experiencing loss first hand makes this tension more real for us than any other difficult experience. It forces us to look past the end of life to eternity while making the present moments we have on earth more meaningful. And that is where we can find happiness.

When we live in light of death, especially with an eye toward eternity, we see life as something given to us, not as something we are entitled to. In this way death actually increases our gratitude, and gratitude increases our enjoyment. We are able to appreciate and revel in all the good things of earth because death reminds us that now is our time to do so. But we will do so with a different perspective than our unbelieving neighbors. If we're trying to hide from death, life will be dominated by these good things as distractions or numbing agents or idols. But if we live with the end in mind, we'll see life as a precious resource—one to be soaked up, shared, and spent in a way that pleases our Creator, prepares us for the next life, and brings others with us into that life.

This is in part why we do not, unlike Siggy Marvin, need to fear death. If we have lived with it as an on-call companion, then death's arrival will not shock or terrify us in the same way. If we have lived with the end in mind, shaping our expectations and directing our decisions, then we will be as prepared as a mortal can be for the end. But this is not an exercise in positive thinking. Living with the end in mind will only free us for happiness if we're living with Jesus in mind, and living in Jesus—saved by him, submitting to him, following him, identified as his... and guaranteed to spend eternity with him on the other side of the grave.

The apostle Paul lived and wrote in light of death more clearly than anyone in the Bible other than Jesus himself. He had such a clear vision of the pending glory and joy of death as a Christian that he went as far as to write, "My desire is to depart and be with Christ, for that is far better" (Philippians 1:23). He yearned to die, but not at the expense of living the life God had given him to the fullest, telling the Christians in Philippi that "to remain in the flesh [that is, stay alive] is more necessary on your account. Convinced of this, I know that I will remain and continue with you all, for your progress and joy in the faith" (v 24-25). His whole attitude is summed up in Philippians 1:21: "To live is Christ, and to die is gain." For Christians, to live is to embody Jesus and fulfill the mission of Jesus. To die is to be with Jesus.

When we are defined by Christ, past and future, we live differently. We are released to be happy within the borders of this mortal life because death defines the boundaries but doesn't finish the game. We are freed and empowered, by the Holy Spirit, to be generous, to serve, to take risks, and to face suffering as Jesus did. We can face the end with assurance that what follows will be better than anything this life has held. That's a profoundly different perspective than one that seeks to fill this life with pleasures to assuage the fear of death, and it's a profoundly happier one.

A DEATH-SHAPED LIFE

The obvious irony in people's manic efforts to avoid death or any thought of death is that by doing so they are lessening their lives. By that I don't mean shortening; that is entirely in God's hands. I mean hollowing. The life lived to avoid and ignore death is void of meaning and purpose. In the movie *The Shawshank Redemption*, the main character, Andy Dufresne, utters a powerful line: "I guess it comes down to a simple choice really; get busy living or get busy dying." Herein lies the irony: when people seek to avoid death, they are getting busy dying. By facing the reality of death from the safety of being saved through Jesus, we can truly get busy living.

To get busy living doesn't necessarily mean that we need to run off and do wild, risky things for Jesus (though it certainly can mean that). It means that the things we're already doing—work, family, church, hobbies, relationships—can be done with a new focus and intentionality. They take on more meaning, not less, because of life's short tenure. They are easier to see as blessings handed to us rather than diversions from a life we can't face. We become caretakers of a precious few years and an invaluable collection of gifts rather than escapees from life's fear and pain.

David Gibson puts it like this: "If you are in denial of death, what is there to do but eat and laugh and drink and party? Instead of being superficial, death invites you to be a person of depth. Only someone who knows how to weep will really know what it means to laugh" (*Living Life Backward*, p 98). The realism of death and the brevity of life concentrate and distill our happiness. When we are not living for pleasure, our pleasure is enlivened and enriched. When we live with death as a backdrop, our lives shine brighter and stand out more clearly. In this we find a new kind of laughter that draws on happiness—one that is purer and deeper.

But we can't do that without *both* of Paul's perspectives. Paul said "to live is Christ"—and he got busy living. But he followed that with "to die is gain," and unless we believe this with all our hearts, we can't truly live. In Christ, death holds no fear for us. It holds an upgrade—an infinite, indescribable improvement in every way. For a follower of Jesus, death is a reward, not a cost. It hurts those who are still living on earth to lose a loved one, but it transports and transforms the one who has died into the presence of God. Part of getting busy living is being eager for that, and that eagerness feeds our enjoyment on this earth. Every pleasure we experience here points to the next life. And the promise of the next life gets us through any pain.

CHAPTER 9

DOES GOD WANT ME TO BE HAPPY?

God wants you to be happy.

This can be a difficult statement to believe. Some of us have a false conception of happiness that pits it against godliness. (I'll tackle this in the next chapter.) Some of us have encountered enough trouble and pain in our lives that it's difficult to see how God could want happiness for us and still let all that stuff happen. And sometimes it's just hard to believe that God loves us in a way such that he smiles on us, is pleased with us, and wants deep happiness for us. Our sin and shame get in the way. We believe the lies of the devil instead. (*You don't measure up. You need to do more to please God. You've sinned too much for God to love you.*)

Over the years I've believed each of these lies at times. I have seen happiness as a distraction from holiness, which made obeying God drudgery instead of a joy. I have looked to heaven in the midst of painful times and wondered what God wanted from me or for me. I have been certain that my failures and my sins ruled me out of ever experiencing the pleasure and smile of God—he might forgive-ish, but I couldn't truly be restored to happy sonship. Even as I write this, I have twinges of uncertainty about whether he truly wants me to be happy. It's so hard to grasp tightly and believe with confidence.

But it is true. God wants me to be happy. He wants you to be happy. To believe otherwise is to turn our backs on a perfect loving Father who stands with arms open to embrace us as his children, and to usher us into the inheritance of joy that he has for us. Yes, in this life we will have trouble. Yes, the specter of death hangs over every living moment. But God is infinitely wise, infinitely good, and infinitely loving, and what we see as insurmountable to our happiness is not even a speed bump to him. It may even be a tool he is using to increase our happiness, as he brings his perfect plans to fruition in his perfect timing.

If you're like me and struggle to have confidence in God's love for you, then this chapter is for you. Throughout Scripture God declares his love for us clearly and lavishly as he proclaims victory over sin and all its effects, including shame and pain and death. We have to work very hard to ignore God's desire for our best. Few passages make it as beautifully, worshipfully obvious as Psalm 16.

> *Preserve me, O God, for in you I take refuge.*
> *I say to the LORD, "You are my Lord;*
> *I have no good apart from you."*
> *As for the saints in the land, they are the excellent ones,*
> *in whom is all my delight.*
> *The sorrows of those who run after another god shall multiply;*
> *their drink offerings of blood I will not pour out*
> *or take their names on my lips.*
> *The LORD is my chosen portion and my cup;*
> *you hold my lot.*

The lines have fallen for me in pleasant places;
    indeed, I have a beautiful inheritance.
I bless the LORD who gives me counsel;
    in the night also my heart instructs me.
I have set the LORD always before me;
    because he is at my right hand, I shall not be shaken.
Therefore my heart is glad, and my whole being rejoices;
    my flesh also dwells secure.
For you will not abandon my soul to Sheol,
    or let your holy one see corruption.
You make known to me the path of life;
    in your presence there is fullness of joy;
    at your right hand are pleasures forevermore.

HAPPINESS FROM GOD

This psalm was written by King David as a song of worship for the people of Israel, and now, through Christ, all God's people are invited to join in. Let's walk through it and pause at different points to enjoy the truths it holds.

I have no good apart from you. (v 2)

From the start, David declares that God is the source and location of all good in life. He doesn't just find good in *trusting* God or *obeying* God, as though God's goodness were some sort of reward for David's actions. No—true happiness, all good, is with and in God himself. There is no good anywhere else. Goodness originates in him and emanates from him. This means that every time God calls a person to repent and believe and become part of his family, he is calling us to *good*—and each subsequent call to repentance, faith and obedience in the course of our Christian life is a call to good too. A summons to God has a built-in promise that it is for our good and for our happiness.

97

One of the ways in which this goodness emanates and spreads is *through* God's people: the "saints in the land" (v 3). Like David we can delight in those who are God's as we live in relationship with them in the church.

The sorrows of those who run after another god shall multiply.
(v 4)

David juxtaposes the promise of God's goodness with the certainty of sorrow if we look elsewhere. We might think of Hinduism, Islam, or Buddhism as pursuing "other gods," and that's true. But we also need a broader understanding of how we're *all* prone to do this. Anything we devote our hearts to, or find our value in, or in which we pursue lasting joy is a god for us—an idol. We run after other gods all the time, be they love, money, success, fitness, or any number of other things we think will bring us lasting happiness. But what David says is crystal clear: any pursuit that becomes worship of anything other than the true God will not just bring about sorrow but will *multiply* our sorrows.

You hold my lot ... indeed, I have a beautiful inheritance.
(v 6)

"That's just my lot in life" is usually said with a heavy dose of resignation. Like a guy who's experienced a series of disappointing relationships and says it's his "lot in life" to be single, or a woman who drops another few hundred dollars to repair her lemon of a car and says it's her "lot in life" to be poor. David uses a similar phrase, but without any sense of fatalism. Our lot in life—what we've received, what we've become, what direction our life is going in—is not in the hands of time or fate or bad luck but in the hands of a personal and sovereign God. This means our lot is the opposite of defeat—it is victory and blessing. In God we have a beautiful inheritance—a rich future of eternal life and joy as his children.

I have set the LORD always before me; because he is at my right hand, I shall not be shaken. (v 8)

In the middle of this psalm of rejoicing, David acknowledges the hardship of life. He is not swept away in ecstasy nor has he lost touch with reality. He knows there will be trouble, and yet he is tied to the Lord and therefore is tied to happiness in the midst of anything that might otherwise shake him.

We have such a propensity for forgetting God and turning elsewhere for hope and help. So like David, we must "set the LORD always before" us—in our minds, our hearts, our meditations, our habits. When we do this, we will begin to recognize God's constant presence. He is there whether we notice him or not, but it is in our awareness that we find comfort and feel safe whatever the trials and quakes of life.

My whole being rejoices; my flesh also dwells secure. (v 9)

David will not let us think that the pleasure and joy of this psalm is only for the after life. When things are not going well in life, it's easy to think, "If I just hold on through this life, I will arrive at that happy heavenly place someday." That's not a wrong hope to hold on to; and sometimes, in our moments of greatest despair, it will be the only hope we have. But if we're tempted to write off any goodness in this life, David's words serve as a corrective. When he writes of our "whole being" and "flesh," he means this mortal life that we are in *now*. We get to have peace and rejoice *now*. We are secure *now*. We have happiness *now* in God. We can have happiness in the midst of trouble and security from that trouble, because we know that those who are in Christ will not be "abandoned" to the grace (v 10).

You make known to me the path of life; in your presence there is fullness of joy; at your right hand are pleasures forevermore.
(v 11)

This verse moves us from our present life to our eternal life with God. And just look at the words David uses. Joy. Pleasures. Fullness. Forever. These words are jackhammers of happiness, shattering our misconceptions and breaking down the false barriers we have put around the truth that God wants us to be happy. He has given us all we need to find happiness: himself. And not just sparse or fleeting happiness. In his presence is joy without lack or flaw. With him there is no end to pleasure.

In this life, we need security and protection and comfort and healing; God provides it. In the next life, we will have perfect eternal peace and security. In this life, we must strive and battle to keep God always before us, in our consciousness. In the next life, he will surround us, and there will be no barrier or temptation or distraction keeping us from him. The psalm ends where it began but with an exclamation! We have no good apart from God, but with God we have good that overflows—fullness of joy and pleasures forevermore.

HABITS (AND REWARDS) OF HAPPINESS

In his book *The Power of Habit* (Random House, 2014), Charles Duhigg describes how pretty much every decision people make is based on the reward we think it will lead to. Over time these decisions can become habitual as we come to expect the rewards they'll bring. This means that if we want to change our habits, we need to redefine the rewards. Then, when we find ourselves carrying out a particular habit because we want a certain reward, we need to adjust our actions toward the new reward.

Duhigg uses the example of cookies. Every afternoon he would start craving a cookie, and then get up from his desk to get one. He realized this wasn't a very healthy habit. So he changed the reward. In this case, the reward became the sense of satisfaction at not getting a cookie and physically feeling better. Then each afternoon when the craving kicked in, Duhigg intentionally got up from his desk and walked a lap around the office. Over time, it worked. His mind and body responded and the desire for cookies diminished, while health and satisfaction increased.

What has this to do with Psalm 16 and eternal joy, you ask?

In the first portion of this book we took a long look at all the ways we pursue happiness where it can't be found. We seek rewards that are temporal and ultimately disappointing—the thrills of going on vacation, living for the next promotion, or gaining the praise of neighbors for a perfectly manicured lawn. Or we seek the reward of safety by eschewing anything that might cause disappointment— avoiding long-term commitments, ducking or exiting from challenging relationships, or turning down promising job opportunities that entail risk. Either way, our habits (the things we do) are bent toward the "reward" of incomplete happiness—a "cookie," if you like—not fullness of joy and pleasures forevermore.

But if we set our minds on a different reward—a heavenly one—our habits will change, and we'll get happier too. Instead of habitually turning to distractions to fill emotional voids, we'll turn to Scripture. Instead of pursuing our value in people's impression of us, we'll pursue a life that God is pleased with. Instead of expecting lasting happiness from temporal things, we'll grow in gratitude for those things as gifts from God.

This is what David describes when he says, "I have set the LORD always before me." He is deciding, over and over again, to prioritize the realities of God and make them his place of peace and security and happiness. This is not a one-time decision but a matter of building new habits by looking to the truest rewards—the peace and happiness God gives now, and the complete joy and pleasure we will enter into when we reach heaven.

This mindset is how we weather the travails and pains of life. By looking at the rewards God offers—his presence, his security, his good gifts—we gain motivation in perseverance. We grow in certainty that God *does* want us to be happy. And in that certainty, we find even greater joy, peace, and fortitude. For if God wants us to be happy, there is nothing to stop us from casting ourselves into his ready and loving arms, now and forever.

CHAPTER 10

HAPPINESS *AND* HOLINESS

As a society, we don't excel at nuance. This means that many cleverly stated falsehoods go unchecked. We especially love a good false dichotomy, particularly if it rhymes or is alliterated. It matters less if it's true than if it's memorable.

One such statement that has laid waste to many people's happiness, and even their faith, is some version of "God wants you to be holy, not happy." While some might put it that bluntly, more often it is applied to specific areas of life. "Marriage isn't about your happiness but your holiness." "Church doesn't exist to make you happy; it exists to make you holy." "It's a parent's job to lead their children toward holiness, not happiness."

This sentiment, however it is expressed, is closely related to the evangeliguilt I described earlier in the book. In fact, in many ways it's the root of it. The guilt we feel for experiencing pleasure is born of the belief that to chase after happiness is to run away from God. This isn't to say we can never be happy, but rather that happiness is, at best, a temporary and surprising circumstantial by-product of doing what is right. We can desire and run after happiness or holiness but not both.

Here's the rub: there is simply no way that this can be true and the last chapter can be true at the same time. A brief definition of holiness is: growing in Christ-likeness through the Holy Spirit's work in our lives so that we pursue the things of God. So, if it's true that God wants us to be happy, then pursuing the things of God cannot be in opposition to happiness.

So why is this false dichotomy so prevalent and so powerful in the lives of so many churches and believers?

THE WRONG KIND OF HAPPINESS

The movie *The Princess Bride* contains a memorable exchange between self-important criminal mastermind Vizzini and Inigo Montoya, the revenge-driven Spanish swordsman. Vizzini repeatedly uses the word "inconceivable." Everything that surprises him is "inconceivable." After numerous such exclamations, Inigo looks sidelong at him and says, "You keep using that word. I do not think it means what you think it means." This is how I feel every time I hear someone pit happiness against holiness. The only way happiness and holiness can be put at odds is to misdefine them both.

We do this, first, by cheapening happiness and reducing it to something trite. The "happiness" that stands in opposition to holiness is cheap, flimsy, and temporary. It is the kind that is found in things of little significance that we think will fulfill us but really won't last—the kind of happiness that we hang on weak hooks and with wrong expectations.

Certainly there is a bastardized version of happiness that can be found in sin too. Pornography arouses. Gluttony satiates. Laziness relaxes. Drunkenness stimulates or numbs, depending on what we need it to medicate. Sexual promiscuity is enthralling and ecstatic. Workaholism gives a sense of accomplishment. Gossip titillates. Criticism leaves us feeling superior.

While the feelings last, that is. Then comes the inevitable crash, leaving us with a need for another hit to keep the high going. And every high is lower than the last, so we increase our intake. In the end we are as strung out emotionally and spiritually as a heroin addict is physically and mentally. What we thought of as happiness was mere emotional self-manipulation.

This kind of "happiness" looks nothing like the joy we saw in Psalm 16, or the pleasure of enjoying every good and perfect gift. It's not the happiness we have when we expect the right things of the right things—a solid, grounded happiness that's earthly but not worldly, and is simply *good*.

So in one sense, to pit this twisted type of "happiness" against holiness is biblically right; it is in opposition to pursuing the things of God. But to call this "happiness" is inaccurate and leads people to believe that pursuing things of God reduces enjoyment in life.

Nothing could be further from the truth.

HOLINESS WITHOUT HAPPINESS

Misdefining happiness is only half the problem. Misdefining holiness is the other half. At least part of the reason we do this is because we've already misunderstood happiness. Once we reduce happiness to something that is opposed to godliness, we end up seeing holiness as a dry husk: a matter of suppressing our desire for the sake what is right. We know there's a reward in heaven—a significant reward to be sure, but it offers a bleak outlook for enjoyment during the duration of our lifetime.

If we remove happiness from holiness, pursuing the things of God becomes drudgery. It is a grind. We become like Sisyphus, the figure from Greek mythology who was cursed to push a boulder up a hill only to see it roll down again, day after day after day for his whole life. We become driven by a sense of moral dread and the burden of obligation. Holiness becomes a word we loathe rather than the wondrous calling and invitation that it actually is in Christ. We mustn't miss the fact that God says that the pursuit of joy is a pursuit of holiness. Remember the command to "Rejoice in the Lord always; again I will say, rejoice" (Philippians 4:4), or "Rejoice in the LORD, O you righteous" (Psalm 97:12), and the significant number of times Jesus says to rejoice (e.g. Matthew 5:12; Luke 10:20; Luke 15:6). Consider that in Galatians joy is listed among the fruit of the Spirit. We are *commanded* to be joyful and told that joy will be a result of life as a follower of Jesus.

Some of you may be a bit uncomfortable right now because you have come to believe that joy and happiness are distinctly different. In this line of thinking, happiness is a temporary, trite emotion, while joy is altogether different—a deep, lasting, rooted, and significant spiritual virtue. So, the thinking goes, *joy* is our reward for holiness, and *happiness* is something unreliable and mostly devoid of spiritual significance.

Let me pose a question in response. What would you think of a person who perpetually promoted joy, spoke of pursuing joy, and expressed the deep riches of joy, but simply didn't seem *happy*? That would be very confusing, right? It would seem at odds and maybe even hypocritical. That's because joy without happiness is nothing but a theological description, at least if it remains that way. Joy that doesn't bring about happiness isn't genuine joy. This doesn't mean that we will always feel happy. And it doesn't mean that happiness will always come easily. Our peace and wholeness and comfort in the Lord will not always immediately bring about laughter and rejoicing. But real biblical joy is always moving us toward those things.

It's true that the Bible says little about the word "happiness." And of course, Scripture commands us to rejoice, making clear that this is much more than a mere feeling—it's something we can choose rather than something we passively experience. But another biblical word helps us understand the connection between happiness and joy: gladness. This is a feeling of pleasure attached to joy: an uplifting of spirit, a bubbling up of *happiness*. Scripture describes serving the Lord with "joyfulness and gladness" (Deuteronomy 28:47), people being "glad of heart for all the goodness that the LORD had shown" (1 Kings 8:66), and people having "light and gladness and joy and honor" (Esther 8:16). Psalm 32:11 rounds out the picture by saying, "Be glad in the LORD, and rejoice." Gladness is paired with joy and rejoicing; it is the feeling that stems from them and fuels them.

This means that when joy in the Lord is lived out, it breeds happiness—the Psalm-16, every-perfect-gift-with-right-expectations kind of happiness that is rich and deep and profound. This is the sort of happiness that is capable of mourning with those who mourn and living realistically under the weight of a fallen world, because it's rooted and realistic. It can comfort the sorrowful and lift up the weary rather than badgering them with trite chipperness and insisting that they look on the bright side of life. It's happiness that reflects God's holiness rather than diminishing it, because if joy is our reward for pursuing holiness, then so is happiness.

HAPPINESS THROUGH HOLINESS

Having said all that, our pursuit of holiness will still involve work because of our sinful nature. It takes effort and discipline. But for those who are in Christ, this effort is done in the power of the Holy Spirit:

> *Therefore, my beloved, as you have always obeyed, so now, not only as in my presence but much more in my absence, work out your own salvation with fear and trembling, for it is God who works in you, both to will and to work for his good pleasure. (Philippians 2:12-13)*

We work for godliness, but it is God who works in us. It takes effort by us, but God is the mover and accomplisher. What's more, God works in us "for his good pleasure." So, even more than our holiness makes us happy, it makes God happy.

This is vital to understand because it moves us far away from thinking of holiness as drudgery. Yes, it is work. Yes, we will fail. Yes, we must persevere. *But* it is God who works in us, and he delights to give us the Holy Spirit, who teaches and empowers us, and enables us to move toward holiness (Luke 11:13). This is a new spiritual dimension entirely, and one that reverberates with hope and happiness.

It is amazing how the changing of a single syllable can alter an entire theological argument and even the trajectory of a life. If we change the framework of our thinking from "happiness and holiness" to "happiness *through* holiness," we alter one tiny word and literally everything else in life follows suit. Instead of happiness and holiness being pitted against one another, they become interdependent. No longer do we have to choose between doing the work of following Jesus or pursuing happiness. Instead we find that pursuing holiness, in all areas of life, through the power of the Holy Spirit, under the smile of God, is where true happiness is to be found.

To put it a different way, pursuing holiness pays off—in this life. As we pursue holiness, "we walk in the light" (1 John 1:7). We step out of spiritual darkness, where we hid in shame and guilt and frustration and loneliness, and we step into the light of Jesus with all our sinful junk. And that's where we find freedom. Freedom to be forgiven over and over again as we fight against sin and still fail. Freedom in the Spirit to pursue the things God loves. Freedom to grow genuine deep relationships. Freedom to enjoy the things of earth as God's good gifts, not as idols. Freedom from the pain that we have inflicted on ourselves or even that others have inflicted on us.

Freedom to keep repenting, knowing that God welcomes all who are in Jesus with open arms.

In the moment, many of these actions feel like sacrifice and self-denial. It's difficult to give up idols because of the prominence we've given them in our lives. It feels humiliating to repent. Turning from habits of sin is hard. Meaningful relationships are risky because vulnerability is frightening. Changing the course of our lives from self-centered to God-oriented can lead us in uncertain directions. But each action is simply denying a self that we left behind when we became Christ's. These actions are risky in that we can still be hurt by fellow sinners, but we know with certainty that we are accepted by God. They involve losses, but only of things by which we no longer want to define ourselves and in which we no longer want to find our worth.

Pursuing holiness is the pursuit of happiness, in this life and the next. Nobody should be happier than a follower of Jesus.

HOLINESS THROUGH HAPPINESS

For a Christian, everything you just read should feel right. We can grow in happiness as we grow in holiness because of the freedom we find in Christ. But we can also grow in holiness as we pursue happiness. It's true. The Bible models to us how.

> *Delight yourself in the LORD,*
> *and he will give you the desires of your heart. (Psalm 37:4)*

This verse begins in such a striking way: with happiness. "*Delight* yourself." Find delight. Then it locates where and how that delight should be: "in the LORD." This is a pursuit of happiness in the things of the Lord. It is freedom to run after all the delight and happiness we can find—in the Lord: in his words, his presence, his people, his gifts, his direction for our lives.

And when we do that, "he will give you the desires of your heart." That does not mean God will give you whatever your heart previously desired. It means that he will give us those delights that we are seeking in him. By pursuing happiness in the Lord, our very desires are reshaped. We want new and different things, which God is pleased to give us lavishly.

To extrapolate from this, it also means we will begin to desire new results from old pleasures. If food was once how we filled the void of loneliness, by delighting ourselves in the Lord we will begin to desire food for enjoyment and out of gratitude. If sex was once how we sought love and validation, by delighting ourselves in the Lord we will begin to see it as the gift God intended for a husband and a wife within the safe and comforting bounds of marriage. If work was once where we found accomplishment and identity, by delighting ourselves in the Lord we will begin to see it as a means of using abilities that he's given us for the purposes of his kingdom.

This means that as we grow in holiness, we are free to pursue happiness because it is ultimately located in the things of God. Our delight in Christian friendship reflects our part in the body of Christ. Our enjoyment of work and creating declares our status as image-bearers. Our pleasure in eating points us to gratitude for God's provision and for the skills of the one who prepared the food. The peace we find in cool breezes and rolling surf is the peace of the Lord shared through his beautiful creation.

God does, indeed, want us to be happy. He wants us to enjoy and to revel and to delight. God wants us to be holy too. What a miracle of his wisdom and love it is, then, that he has given us everything we need to find both.

CHAPTER 11

THE PLEASURE
OF THE PROMISE

Each night when I tuck my kids into bed (or send them to bed, as is the case more often as they get older and are in less need of tucking), I tell them I love them. They tell me they love me too, I turn the lights off, and I head to my easy chair to grab a few moments of quiet. Sometimes they stop me before I make it out the door to ask a question about the mysteries of life or a particularly knotty theological issue because they know full well I can't ignore such questions. But most of the time there is a simple exchange of "I love yous" and then sleep.

You know what never happens when I put them to bed? It never happens that I tell them I love them, give them a hug and kiss, turn to leave their room, and hear, "Do you still love me now?"—as if my love somehow changed or departed in those few seconds. They know that my statement of love was not just true in the moment I said it, but that it was a statement of how I always am toward them. They know that it will be true in the middle of the night, the next morning, and when they are grown and have moved on. Yes, they need assurances and reminders, especially when they screw up. But what they hear in the phrase "I love you" is "I have loved you, I do love you, and I will love you."

How much more should we hear God's words in that way. My love for my children is flawed and incomplete, and demands that I apologize to them often for my failures. Sometimes they need reminders that I love them because I failed to show it well. God never has to repent because he never sins or fails. He doesn't have good days and bad days. He never changes or goes back on his word. And that means that every word God says about himself carries a promise in it.

So when God says something about himself in his word, it is sure to be true, to have been true, and to always be true. When he describes himself, it is a promise. When he speaks of his deeds, it is a promise. When he declares his love or protection or presence, it is a promise. And when he says he will keep his promises, it is a promise.

And it is God's promises, found in Scripture, that are the source of true happiness, that direct our hopes, and that shape our expectations—or at least they should.

So let's take a look at some of them. Promises that God has made and kept in the past; promises that God has made and is bringing about in the present; and promises that God has made and will keep in the future. We won't be able to explore all the promises of God, and it would be madness to even try because there are so many! Instead we'll focus on a selection of promises as hallmarks of God's character to help us see how they define hope, happiness, and expectations for the Christian.

PROMISES PAST

One of our most common sins is forgetfulness. I don't mean the accidental forgetfulness that leaves car keys on the counter or misses a dentist appointment (ok, that was probably a little bit on purpose). I mean the willful amnesia as to what God says about God. We allow ourselves to be blinded by present concerns, temptations, distractions, and wishes, all of which diminish our happiness and drown out the truths of who God is and what he has done. That's why Scripture is so full of reminders of God's faithfulness in history. These "promises past" help remedy our amnesia and constantly nudge us back into alignment with God's way.

We see an example of this in Exodus 3, where we find Moses herding sheep in the wilderness, having fled from Egypt in fear of his life. He stumbles upon a bush that is aflame but is not burning up and realizes quickly that it is a supernatural occurrence—the very presence of God in fact. Out of the burning bush God speaks to Moses and calls him to lead Israel out of captivity. Moses is understandably fearful, and he asks God what he should tell the people about who sent him.

> God said to Moses, "I AM WHO I AM." And he said, "Say this to the people of Israel: 'I AM has sent me to you.'" God also said to Moses, "Say this to the people of Israel: 'The LORD, the God of your fathers, the God of Abraham, the God of Isaac, and the God of Jacob, has sent me to you.' This is my name forever, and thus I am to be remembered throughout all generations. (Exodus 3:14-15)

What a promise! God describes himself as the unchanging one: the one who has always been and the one who always will be. He points back in Israelite history to the patriarchs, and how he was with them and faithful to them. And he calls the people to remember him going forwards. So can Moses and the Israelites trust God's promise to bust them out of slavery? Yes, because he has always been trustworthy, has always been with them in the past, and will not ever change. He points Moses back to give the people faith for the future.

The events that followed this burning-bush encounter—the ten plagues and the exodus of God's people through the Red Sea—is recounted on numerous occasions throughout the rest of the Old Testament. God wanted his people to always remember their rescue from Egypt as a seminal event that proved his power, faithfulness, and rescue. Psalm 106 is one example. In 46 verses the psalmist recounts the drama of the exodus, and then Israel's wilderness journey to the promised land, particularly highlighting the people's sins and rebellion against God. This had eventually caused them to be taken into exile. Yet the psalm begins and ends with "Praise the LORD." It lauds the fact that God is merciful and just and patient, even as his people stumble around in the wilderness, literally or spiritually. So this psalm would have given the Israelites who sang it hope in the face of their failure as they looked to God's character.

In the same way that the people of Israel were defined by God's faithfulness in the exodus, we have our own defining account of God miraculously setting his people free. We look back on the life, death, and resurrection of Jesus. All the promises for the present and the future that you're about to read of only matter because of a past promise, given over centuries throughout the Old Testament and then fulfilled and sealed at the cross. Just as Israel remembered God's rescue at the exodus by celebrating the Passover, we remember God's rescue of sinners by celebrating the Lord's Supper. In that simple act of collectively eating bread and drinking wine, we look back on Christ's rescue and remember its reality in the present.

The whole Bible story speaks of God's promises: from the creation to the formation of God's people, to the founding of their home in the promised land, to the rule of judges and then kings, to the words of prophets, to Israel's exile, to their return, to the coming of Jesus, to the founding of his church; woven through it all are promises. These words of God tell of his faithfulness, his commands, his presence, his power, his love, his justice. They reveal all that God would have us know of his character and deeds and plan. We look back at Scripture not for a light dinner of chicken soup for our souls but to see and know and rest in the reality of God.

PROMISES PRESENT

It is one thing to look back and know that God has been faithful, and find peace in that. And in a moment we'll look ahead and see that God will set things right. But what about now, as we live in this in-between place full of conflicting joys and pains? This reality is why God has given us promises for the present. These words of God shine light into dark days and bring happiness of the purest, rightest, most holy kind.

While God's promises are too deep and profound to be placed neatly into buckets addressing different needs, he does care about our present struggles, and his words are for those moments when life is difficult. So here are just some of God's "promises present" for whatever it is we're feeling or facing.

FEARFUL

While most of us don't go through life fearing for our well-being because of enemies, we all fear people. We fear gossip. We fear injustice. We fear the consequences of doing what's right in the face of injustice. We fear looking foolish and being humiliated. And we need this sort of reminder of just who is in charge and who holds our lives.

God promises:

> The LORD is on my side; I will not fear.
>   What can man do to me? (Psalm 118:6)

WORRIED

We worry about our health or our children's future. We worry about how we'll pay off debts or whether our new business will succeed. We worry that our country is going to hell in a handbasket and taking us all with it. And some days we wake up with a general sense of dread and fear. We control so little of our lives, and it can be paralyzing when we begin to think about all that could happen. God promises:

> Do not be anxious about anything, but in everything by prayer and supplication with thanksgiving let your requests be made known to God. And the peace of God, which surpasses all understanding, will guard your hearts and your minds in Christ Jesus. (Philippians 4:6-7)

CONFUSED

When life is difficult and we are suffering, the first question we ask is "Why?" Why would God ordain things to happen like this? Most of the time we won't get a complete answer to that question. But God does tell us of at least one purpose for every difficulty, and in purpose there is clarity and hope. God promises:

> Blessed be the God and Father of our Lord Jesus Christ, the Father of mercies and God of all comfort, who comforts us in all our affliction, so that we may be able to comfort those who are in any affliction, with the comfort with which we ourselves are comforted by God. For as we share abundantly in Christ's sufferings, so through Christ we share abundantly in comfort too. (2 Corinthians 1:3-5)

OVERWHELMED

When everything has hit the fan and life is too much, God gives us what we need for that too. We can find safety in his strong presence. He gives us pictures of security for us to envision, like this one:

> The name of the LORD is a strong tower;
>   the righteous man runs into it and is safe. (Proverbs 18:10)

SHAME, GUILT AND DOUBT

Some of us need present promises for another sort of struggle—one within our souls. It may be a battle with shame and guilt: the feeling you can never be forgiven for sins you have committed. Or a struggle to feel that God is there at all. Or a feeling of being unworthy, not good enough to be God's child, and wondering if you are really saved. God speaks to us in these struggles as well.

The Lord is merciful and gracious,
slow to anger and abounding in steadfast love. (Psalm 103:8)

If we confess our sins, he is faithful and just to forgive us our
sins and to cleanse us from all unrighteousness. (1 John 1:9)

ALONE

One of the most powerful realities for Christians is that Jesus is advocating for us. He is on our side. He has won us through his death and resurrection, and will not let us go. He is with God, talking to God on our behalf. He is interceding with God, in his own name, for us. And he tells us this so we will know we can be close to God in freedom and peace and happiness.

For we do not have a high priest who is unable to sympathize
with our weaknesses, but one who in every respect has
been tempted as we are, yet without sin. Let us then with
confidence draw near to the throne of grace, that we may
receive mercy and find grace to help in time of need.
(Hebrews 4:15-16)

ONE FINAL CATCH-ALL PROMISE

If you are in a spiritually dark place, then Romans 8 is a wonderful place in which to rest and meditate and pray. You could live in this chapter for days and weeks at a time and never plumb the depths of its goodness for your soul. Here's the culmination of the chapter:

> For I am sure that neither death nor life, nor angels nor rulers, nor things present nor things to come, nor powers, nor height nor depth, nor anything else in all creation, will be able to separate us from the love of God in Christ Jesus our Lord. (Romans 8:38-39)

PROMISES FUTURE

When we think of promises, this is likely the category that comes to mind most readily—the ones that look ahead at better things to come. But as important as these are, they become so much fuller and richer when we consider them in light of promises past and present. Every promise God gives is tied to every other, because they all stem from who he is and what Christ accomplished at the cross.

So here is the picture that one particular passage in Revelation paints of what we can gladly look forward to:

> Then I saw a new heaven and a new earth, for the first heaven and the first earth had passed away, and the sea was no more. And I saw the holy city, new Jerusalem, coming down out of heaven from God, prepared as a bride adorned for her husband. And I heard a loud voice from the throne saying, "Behold, the dwelling place of God is with man. He will dwell with them, and they will be his people, and God himself will be with them as their God. He will wipe away every tear from their eyes, and death shall be no more, neither shall there be mourning, nor crying, nor pain anymore, for the former things have passed away."

> And he who was seated on the throne said, "Behold, I am making all things new." Also he said, "Write this down, for these words are trustworthy and true." And he said to me, "It

is done! I am the Alpha and the Omega, the beginning and the end. To the thirsty I will give from the spring of the water of life without payment. The one who conquers will have this heritage, and I will be his God and he will be my son. But as for the cowardly, the faithless, the detestable, as for murderers, the sexually immoral, sorcerers, idolaters, and all liars, their portion will be in the lake that burns with fire and sulfur, which is the second death." (Revelation 21:1-8)

Reflect on some of these phrases and truths.

"And I saw the holy city, new Jerusalem, coming down out of heaven from God, prepared as a bride adorned for her husband." This shouts of beauty and newness and expectation and joy. We should read it with the anticipation of a groom bouncing on his toes, unable to contain his smile at the woman walking down the aisle to marry him.

"It is done!" On this day God will have finished his perfect work. All the hoping will be behind us because everything will be a fully realized certainty from that day forth and forever.

"He will dwell with them." No more will God seem distant—not that he ever was, but we will see him and know his nearness with certainty. His home will be with us, and we will be his people.

"He will wipe away every tear from their eyes, and death shall be no more, neither shall there be mourning, nor crying, nor pain anymore, for the former things have passed away … I am making all things new." What else could we ask for? All the things that sully or snatch away our happiness will be gone, erased forever. What will replace them will be what was lost at Eden: perfection. We will at last know total, untainted happiness.

"But as for the cowardly, the faithless, the detestable, as for murderers, the sexually immoral, sorcerers, idolaters, and all liars, their portion will be in the lake that burns with fire and sulfur, which is the second death." For seven verses God pours out promise after promise of glory and newness and perfection. But then comes this verse. Why? Because we need this kind of "warning promise." We need the reminder that eternity is for all, but glory is only for those who are Christ's—and so we need to keep going in trusting in him. And we need the reminder that God's glory and power are perfect in judgment and mercy alike.

What a promise this passage holds. What a portrait of perfect happiness. What a hope to cling to in the midst of *anything* we face now.

PROMISES AND HAPPINESS

As we saw in chapter 5, God's promises define reality. They draw the lines of hope and happiness. So we must ask ourselves whether our expectations, our pursuits, and our definition of happiness align with what God has said. When a child yanks out of his parent's grasp in a crowd, runs away, gets lost, and consequently becomes terrified, has the parent's presence and care failed him? Not at all. His own actions led him away from peace and happiness in pursuit of what he thought was better. Similarly, when we feel unhappy and hopeless, it is not because God's promises have failed us or because God has abandoned us but because we have distanced ourselves: we forgot.

True happiness lies in remembering what God has said and done, so that we can rest in the hope of what God will one day do. And we remember by returning to his promises, his words, day after day, for as long as it is called today (Hebrews 3:13).

CHAPTER 12

GROWING IN GROUNDED HAPPINESS

I have a cynical bent that God is slowly straightening. I easily see the downside and ill motives in situations. I get frustrated with bright-eyed optimists who take things at face value, always think the best of people, and believe every story they're told by buskers, toddlers, or salesmen. I usually try to fend off accusations of cynicism by calling myself a "realist," which, in my case, is sort of like a benchwarmer calling himself a "vital reserve player." It is aspirational and not entirely accurate.

But over the years, and with a fair amount of growing pain, I have taken baby steps away from the harsh, acerbic cynicism of youth to a more balanced and biblical view of reality. Bit by bit, Scripture has opened my eyes to an understanding of man's capacity for evil and God's capacity for grace. No book in Scripture has helped me with this more than Ecclesiastes. Picking a favorite book of the Bible is like a parent picking a favorite child; we're not supposed to, but on any given day we usually have one. Ecclesiastes is mine more days than not. My aim in this chapter is to show how this enigmatic, powerful little book of wisdom has shaped and defined biblical happiness for me, in the hope that you will find as much goodness in it as I have.

HOW DOES ECCLESIASTES FIT?

I remember reading Ecclesiastes in both high school and college, and each time having the same reaction: what is this weird book even doing in here? It was simply twelve chapters of confusion. In my mind it became one of those portions of Scripture reserved for checking boxes on a Bible-reading plan.

Years later in the midst of just such a reading plan, I found myself staring into the morass of Ecclesiastes again. Only this time, I began to get it.

What had changed? I had.

Ecclesiastes is part of the scriptural genre called wisdom literature. These are the books of the Bible (Job, Psalms, Proverbs, Ecclesiastes, Song of Solomon) that most clearly speak into common life experiences. They draw on the grist and grind of everyday life to reveal truths about God, and they shine those truths about God onto the grist and grind of everyday life. As I returned to Ecclesiastes a decade or more after that first encounter, I'd lived enough life to have had the shine knocked off me. I'd had enough life experiences, both good and bad, to begin to learn what I didn't know.

Which meant that this time around, Ecclesiastes rang true for me. Here was King Solomon (aka "the Preacher")—one of the wisest and wealthiest men who ever lived—reflecting in his old age on what his life had come to. Here was a man who had many triumphs and glories, but who also made many moral compromises and sinful choices later in life. It was a context that I could understand (despite not being the wisest or wealthiest anything ever) because it was real—with real successes, real enjoyment, real loss, real mistakes, real cost; and I'd had my share of those.

In the years since, I have revisited Ecclesiastes often enough to no longer be a mere guest. I have my own key and am free to let myself in whenever I need a place to stay. It is a home in the midst of Scripture's 66 books. (All the other books are equally hospitable, but I simply find my way back to Ecclesiastes often.) Through life's devastations and joys it speaks balance and steadiness. When I am tempted to place my hopes in something that cannot hold them, it bluntly tells me just how foolish that would be. When I am inclined to pessimism and frustration, it points me to the sincere pleasures and happiness that God has given in this life. Ecclesiastes will neither let me get too high nor too low.

The beauty of a book like this, and all the wisdom literature in Scripture, is that it's for everyone who will listen. You too can find grounded, happy realism in its pages. Here are some of the ways in which Ecclesiastes directs us, shapes us, and offers a paradigm for happiness.

BEWARE OF DEAD ENDS

The words of the Preacher, the son of David, king in
Jerusalem. Vanity of vanities, says the Preacher, vanity of
vanities! All is vanity. (1:1-2)

These opening words of Ecclesiastes certainly don't seem like a very promising beginning for this so-called paradigm for human happiness. Quite the opposite, actually. It feels more like a warning of woe than a promise of bliss. And in a sense it is.

These opening words function a bit like a "road closed" sign. They tell us to reconsider our direction and to take another way. There is an implied "or else" in these words: *You've been pursuing happiness in the wrong way, running after fulfillment in the wrong things. Seek happiness in a different way or else...* Solomon knew the human heart and our proclivity for replacing things of eternal value with things of temporal enjoyment. After all, he was the king bestowed with supernatural wisdom, who still wandered away from the Lord after sex and political alliances and riches. This, he says, is vanity—a vapor.

A warning is where most of us need to start. We are so single-mindedly devoted to pursuing happiness in directions which won't last that the only way to snap us out of our tunnel vision is for the Preacher to rhetorically grab us by the collar and give us a hearty shake. We need our foolish expectations and false hopes set straight. So the Preacher wipes them away in a sentence (and then over and over again throughout the book), not to leave us hopeless but to reconstruct happiness in a manner that reflects the realities of mortal, broken earthly life and eternal, joyful life with God. What Ecclesiastes declares is not, *Happiness is unattainable*, but rather, *Happiness is attainable only if understood and pursued rightly*. Then it shows us how to (and not to) understand and pursue it.

VIEW ALL THINGS IN LIGHT OF ETERNITY

An inescapable theme of Ecclesiastes is that of mortality. We see this in the Preacher's repeated use (26 times in only twelve chapters) of the term "under the sun": a statement of duration, not geography. Just as the sun has always been used to measure times and seasons, here it is being used to define our lifespan. Eventually our day will come to an end; our time under the sun will cease. In fact, *everything* comes to an end eventually. That is what the Preacher means when he calls all things "vanity." It's not that they're meaningless or valueless but that they will not last. From the get-go, the Preacher reframes our perspective to see all of life in light of death.

If this strikes you as uncomfortably morbid, that is precisely why Ecclesiastes is written this way. We hate facing the reality of death. We hate its certainty and its finality. We hate how it robs us of joys. But we cannot escape it, so we must face it. Time and again, Ecclesiastes reflects the bleakness and grief of loss: "How the wise dies just like the fool!" (2:16); "All go to one place. All are from the dust, and to dust all return" (3:20); "This is an evil in all that is done under the sun, that the same event happens to all" (9:3).

Yet we're mistaken if we take the message of Ecclesiastes to be *Well, this life is all there is so enjoy it while you can because nothing else really matters.* In fact, Ecclesiastes points us in an entirely different and better direction. Death, as Ecclesiastes makes clear, puts a necessary limitation on us so that, if we are paying attention, we don't make eternal idols out of temporal experiences. And for followers of Jesus, death is not the end of happiness. In fact, it is the end of suffering and pain, and an entry into the presence of the Lord, at whose right hand are pleasures forevermore. So rather than thinking of death as the thief of joy, we are corrected to think of life in light of this invitation to perfect joy.

VALUE THINGS FOR WHAT GOD CREATED THEM TO BE

As you read Ecclesiastes and begin to see life in light of eternity, another shift begins to take place. The pieces of life that we put our hopes in most often—relationships, work, wealth, health, etc.—come into clearer focus. Some of them—those we have made too much of—recede to a place of less prominence. Others—those we have overlooked and been unappreciative of—begin to take on greater and more appropriate value.

God created innumerable good gifts and blessings for us, but we fail to enjoy them as we ought because we have placed far too much or far too little value on them. By attending to life with eternity in mind, we are able to see and value them as God intends us to. We see this in Ecclesiastes 5:18 and 9:9:

> *Behold, what I have seen to be good and fitting is to eat and drink and find enjoyment in all the toil with which one toils*

under the sun the few days of his life that God has given him, for this is his lot. (5:18)

Enjoy life with the wife whom you love, all the days of your vain life that he has given you under the sun, because that is your portion in life and in your toil at which you toil under the sun. (9:9)

The same is true for circumstances of a negative sort too. Life is full of suffering and loss, and we are often overwhelmed by it to the point of despair. If we encounter suffering in light of eternity, though, we see it as God intended us to. It does not become less painful, but it does become less powerful—a "light momentary affliction," as Paul writes in 2 Corinthians 4:17.

FEAR THE LORD AND BE GRATEFUL
Ecclesiastes ends with these words:

The end of the matter; all has been heard. Fear God and keep his commandments, for this is the whole duty of man. For God will bring every deed into judgment, with every secret thing, whether good or evil. (Ecclesiastes 12:13-14)

After twelve chapters of complexity and exhortation and reflection, the Preacher boils the conclusion down to this: "Fear God and keep his commandments."

In doing this, we will arrive at genuine happiness. Consider, for example, God's commands to rejoice and be thankful:

Rejoice in the Lord always; again I will say, rejoice.
                                        (Philippians 4:4)

Give thanks to the LORD, for he is good. (Psalm 107:1)

So to be grateful is to obey God's commands—and to act in a manner worthy of a holy God. What is more, fearing the Lord actually moves us into gratitude, because it acknowledges his rightful, holy place above all of life and all of time—and how little we're entitled to and yet how much we have. By fearing we become grateful, by being grateful we obey God's commands, and in both we find happiness.

Indeed, fearing the Lord is the lens through which to view the whole of Ecclesiastes. It is the tone, the foundation, and the outcome of the entire book. To view life with eternity in mind is to fear the Lord, because we acknowledge his infinity and the beauty of eternal life with him. To have right expectations is to fear the Lord, because we submit to his standards rather than creating our own. It also fuels our gratitude because we are able to enjoy life in the manner in which he intended us to, with an eye toward the life he promises to all who follow him. These closing words of Ecclesiastes are rich with the promise of happiness.

HAPPINESS DEFINED

What Ecclesiastes leaves a careful reader with is not a sense of ecstasy or bliss. It is not a book of excitement or thrills or giddiness. There are not even any "pinnacle passages" like those you find elsewhere in Scripture. Ecclesiastes spends more time talking about unhappiness than happiness. And yet I find this little book to be foundational for human happiness. It does not take us to the pinnacle of happiness; it sets a baseline. It is not a how-to book; it sets boundaries. It does not give ingenious strategies; it sets the rules. So if you haven't read Ecclesiastes in a while, or maybe ever, why not pick it up and give it a try?

Most people go through life looking for peak happiness, always seeking to increase the sensation and up the experience. Ecclesiastes wants no part in that and warns against it. Rather it defines happiness in a manner that is realistic and accessible. It offers a grounded version of happiness that we can hold onto throughout the difficulties of life.

This side of heaven, what else can we ask for? In fact, we've already asked for it. We've sought it. We've chased it. And we've come up empty. Happiness is life's most elusive feeling. But we've seen that it can become both a present and a lasting reality.

Why? Because God wants you to be happy.

He is a generous Father, who showers you with good things day by day and invites you to enjoy them freely, daily, for your pleasure.

He is a God who speaks to you and whose words define reality and can shape your expectations, if you will listen, so that you live your life with hopeful, grounded realism.

He is a good shepherd, who walks with you, leads you, and works in you through the deep valleys and rocky parts of life; who sent his Son to die and rise again so that all his promises of salvation are yours.

And he is the eternal sovereign ruler of the universe, who will one day bring about a new creation that will be set free from sin and sorrow, where the people of God will experience pure, untainted joy as we gladly worship our Savior.

So hang your happiness on the right hooks, hang your hopes on God's promises, fear him, and obey his commands—and in this you'll find happiness, now and forever.

FOUR FINAL QUESTIONS

Nobody likes a book that ends with an unnecessary chapter of simplistic application. (Well, actually, lots of people seem to like them, given the sales numbers of many such books.) Needless to say, I don't like them, so I am going to wrap this one up with something that I hope is more helpful—and the kind of resource you can revisit from time to time.

The questions that follow are ones with which I have wrestled in the writing of this book, and which I continue to think about regularly. I hope these final thoughts will help you to find real happiness and rest in it.

WHAT IS THE DIFFERENCE BETWEEN JOY AND HAPPINESS?

Many Christians think of joy as deeply spiritual and virtuous, and think of happiness as experiential, untrustworthy, and fleeting. Joy is rooted and unshakable while happiness lives on the whim of a mood and the serendipity of circumstance. As we saw in chapter 10, these definitions are unhelpful and cause people unnecessary turmoil.

Certainly, people can have a version of happiness without having joy in the Lord. Temporal happiness is all around us all the time. Happiness, in this sense, is not within the purview of Christians alone. Matthew 5:45 tells us that God "makes his sun rise on the evil and on the good, and sends rain on the just and on the unjust," so it's clear that the good gifts of God are enjoyed by all people to some degree. People eat and drink. People fall in love. People marvel at the beauty of the Matterhorn or an Edgar Degas oil painting. But this happiness—a tug toward the eternal—is incomplete. It is meant to lift people's eyes to the things of God. Instead most people make their way through life moving from one temporal happiness to another.

This version of happiness is the beginning of something lasting and magnificent. But without an eye toward the eternal, it is happiness without joy—a fleeting pursuit of the next good feeling. However good it looks on the surface, at its root it is idolatrous and dangerous.

So you can have a version of happiness without joy, but you cannot have genuine joy without happiness. To be joyful is to be glad, to rejoice, to be grateful, to be at peace. Joy should be magnetic and compelling, not life in the doldrums. In short, to be joyful is to be *happy* in those things that are lasting and transformative. A professed joy that lacks happiness is nothing but an articulated belief system, and it is hypocrisy.

When we recognize the inextricable wovenness of genuine happiness and joy, it relieves us of a burden of unnecessary guilt over *enjoyment* in life's pleasures (evangeliguilt). It gives us permission to—and even compels us to—find laughter and peace in the midst of life's worst circumstances. The complex reality of human emotion is that we rarely experience just one feeling at a time. We find that we can be truly happy in the midst of suffering even though we are grieving and burdened because of the suffering. We don't need to extricate our joy from our happiness or put one on a spiritual pedestal while the other plays in the yard. To do so is to falsify both.

IS UNHAPPINESS SIN? HOW ABOUT UNHAPPINESS IN THE MIDST OF SUFFERING?

Well, that depends.

In chapter 4 we took a long look at how we live under a curse because of sin. Nothing is as it is supposed to be. And every human knows this at a visceral and often subconscious level. We *feel* the wrongness of injustice, unkindness, illness, brokenness, and death. They make us unhappy, and this unhappiness is a reflection of God's image in us. We are designed to abhor what is evil, what is wrong, what shouldn't be. This kind of unhappiness is right.

This means that when we suffer, we are free to lament—to grieve but with faith that God is in control. We should abhor the pain that a cursed reality has brought about. We ought to yearn for resolution, for healing, for justice, and ultimately for the return of Jesus to set things right. The Gospels tell of Jesus weeping over the death of a friend, mourning over the plight of a city he loved, and pleading with God for a way out of the suffering of crucifixion. He was rightly unhappy with the devastation wrought by sin.

But he was never selfish. His unhappiness did not turn to complaint, to blaming, to bad moods, or to mistrust of his Father. Just the opposite. When Jesus asked, "Father, all things are possible for you. Remove this cup from me," in the same breath he prayed, "Yet not what I will, but what you will" (Mark 14:36). He was unhappy, but trusting. He was unhappy, but obedient. He was unhappy, but he did not let it direct him away from the course God had called him to.

Our unhappiness becomes sinful when it focuses on the self. We instinctively do this *all* the time—and the effects can be devastating. We allow the brokenness in one area of life to splatter its acid all over other areas of life, so that we become blind to that for which we should be thankful. Or we experience a wrong of some kind, and our reaction is disproportionate and causes even more wreckage. Or we wallow in unhappiness, as if that will somehow make us happier, rather than seeking the happiness Christ offers through his Spirit and through so many good gifts.

Unhappiness is part of life until we go to meet Jesus or he returns. We will never be completely happy, completely satisfied, or permanently at peace in this life. And this does not have to be sinful. In fact, it can be God-honoring as we respond to life's unhappiness in the manner Jesus did—selflessly, joyfully trusting God and pressing on.

ARE MY EXPECTATIONS RIGHT, REALISTIC, AND GODLY?

So much of happiness is tied to what we expect. But how do we know if what we expect is *right*? Here are some filters we can run expectations through to help ourselves determine if they are realistic and God-honoring.

Who are my expectations benefiting? The easiest thing in the world is to think of ourselves first and only. It is our sinful nature to prioritize ourselves at the cost of anyone else, and it is contrary to everything Scripture teaches about serving others, considering their needs, bearing with one another, and taking up our crosses as followers of Jesus. If the primary, or only, beneficiary of your expectations is yourself, you need to consider how they align with what God says is right and true.

When you head into a relationship, are you thinking primarily of how it will be good for you or how it will be good for the other person? When you join a church, are you considering only what it offers you or what you can bring to it? In any decision, are you considering the cost to yourself or only the benefit? Are you willing to absorb that cost for the good of others, even if it is unpleasant? And have you considered how the benefit to you might actually be a cost to others?

Who do I depend on to meet my expectations? This question goes hand in hand with the one above. It is impossible to have expectations that truly depend on God and are also self-centered in their outcome. To depend on God (to "fear God," Ecclesiastes 12:13) is to put him first. When we do this, it rearranges or replaces our selfish motivations and orients us toward expectations that truly please God. When we have expectations that are selfish, we can be sure that they are dependent on ourselves, or other people, to fulfill them.

That's not to say we don't need other people or that leaning on them is wrong. God has designed us for relationships in which we depend on one another. But there is a significant difference between the kind of depending on people that puts all our faith in them and the kind that recognizes *their* need for God to empower and enable them. The former places a burden of expectation on people that will inevitably lead to disappointment. The second acknowledges their God-given abilities and capacities with gratitude, while resting in God's ongoing work through them. This is freeing and gracious.

When our expectations are God-dependent, they become God-defined. We simply can't expect God to do anything that God didn't say he would do. Remembering this keeps us from hoping for things that dishonor God, while enabling us to expect remarkable, mind-blowing things from God by faith. We often will not know what to hope for or expect in particular situations, but when we depend on God, we know that he will do what is best—whether or not our expectations come to fruition. When we depend on ourselves, or on others, we risk becoming proud or embittered, depending on whether our expectations were met or not.

What do I know of the one I am depending on? When we depend on God, we know that our expectations are in perfect hands—but they are also in mysterious ones. God will do things we never thought possible and that we never asked for. His wisdom is too great and wonderful for us, so we will never know the full picture of why and how he does what he does. However, if we know him well—his character, his word, his promises—we will find peace and happiness in the outcomes he gives. If we don't have a firm grasp on God's character, we'll struggle to believe and find peace in outcomes we did not expect or want.

When we depend on people, even in a healthy way, we need to be equally aware of who they are—fallen image-bearers of God with an incredible capacity for both good and evil. We are fools if we don't let this shape our expectations of people. They can bring us great joy and do us real good, but they will inevitably let us down too. There is only one person who works for our good in all things, all the time—and it's not our spouse, or our friend, or our pastor (Romans 8:28). This is why we depend on God even as we depend on people. It is only through God's work that people do good and can be trusted. Another way to put it would be: who does the one you depend on depend on?

HOW DO I ENJOY LIFE WITHOUT GUILT? HOW DO I KEEP ENJOYMENT FROM BECOMING IDOLATRY?

One of the main reasons I wrote this book was because I was tired of wrestling with guilt over having fun and enjoying myself. It seemed strange that God would give so many wonderful gifts only for me to feel guilty for enjoying them. On the other hand, I could also recognize my propensity for turning good things into idols, and that wasn't ok either. Thus began my efforts at wrestling these tensions into a (hopefully) coherent and biblically faithful book. In the spirit of Ecclesiastes, and hopefully with a dash of Solomon's wisdom, I'll conclude with the following thoughts.

Be grateful in everything. If you acknowledge and thank the source of your blessings, it is so much harder to turn them into idols of any kind.

Appreciate good gifts as God intended. Savor the delicious things. Laugh at the humorous things. Thrill at the exhilarating things. Enjoy the entertaining things. Cheer at the joyous things. Ponder the deep things. Rest in the peaceful things. Reflect on the somber things. Wonder at the beautiful things. Cherish the precious things. And share them all, for happiness is multiplied when gifts are experienced together.

Live the life God has given you to the fullest. Imagine taking a child to the playground. If she continually came back asking, "Am I swinging right?" or "Am I sliding right?" you would eventually say, "Just go play! Enjoy yourself. Have fun." We are like that child when we worry too much about *how* to enjoy life rather than simply being fully engaged and enjoying it.

Repent often and eagerly. We will get things wrong dozens of times every day for the rest of our lives. We will sin in our hearts, minds, and actions. We can either let our sins drive us from God, or we can remember the work of Christ and take our sins to God, our good Father, who stands ready to forgive us and is generous with good gifts. When we repent, the Holy Spirit changes us, by degrees, toward holiness, where perfect peace and happiness are found.

Fear God and keep his commandments. These words are the final instruction of the Preacher in Ecclesiastes, and they are the perfect summation of our pursuit of happiness. "The fear of the LORD is the beginning wisdom" (Proverbs 9:10). It is the grounds for all gratitude. It is the orientation of our hearts to truth and right expectations. It is dependence and honor and trust. From it flows a desire to keep God's commandments because we see them as life-giving and good. In God's words we have freedom to enjoy, strength to overcome, and a promise of true happiness.

the good book
COMPANY

BIBLICAL | RELEVANT | ACCESSIBLE

At The Good Book Company, we are dedicated to helping Christians and local churches grow. We believe that God's growth process always starts with hearing clearly what he has said to us through his timeless word—the Bible.

Ever since we opened our doors in 1991, we have been striving to produce Bible-based resources that bring glory to God. We have grown to become an international provider of user-friendly resources to the Christian community, with believers of all backgrounds and denominations using our books, Bible studies, devotionals, evangelistic resources, and DVD-based courses.

We want to equip ordinary Christians to live for Christ day by day, and churches to grow in their knowledge of God, their love for one another, and the effectiveness of their outreach.

Call us for a discussion of your needs or visit one of our local websites for more information on the resources and services we provide.

Your friends at The Good Book Company

thegoodbook.com | thegoodbook.co.uk
thegoodbook.com.au | thegoodbook.co.nz
thegoodbook.co.in